PN Review 234

VOLUME 43   NUMBER 4   MARCH–APRIL 201

Editorial

THE ECOLOGY OF poetry publishing is fragile. At the moment, to those of us active in the field, it seems alarmingly so. Among the large players Fulcrum and Menard, and among the smaller Peterloo, Mandeville, Sycamore and many others have come and gone in living memory. Almost twenty years ago Oxford University Press closed its poetry list. Other commercially-based lists diminished, vanished; a few have reappeared: for how long? Publishing poetry by living writers and trying to keep faith with them devolves upon shoestring independents – Arc, Bloodaxe, Carcanet, Eyewear, Shearsman, to name few – and a brave band of very little presses. Large and small, built by individuals with editorial flair, they come, make a difference, and – inexorably – go.

In this issue of *PN Review* (News & Notes) we bid adieu to CB Editions, which has achieved great things in its decade. Last year Anvil, a major player in British poetry publishing for half a century, with important discoveries to its credit and a mighty translation list, merged its activities with those of Carcanet, and Peter Jay, poet and translator as well as a notable editor and book designer, retired. Like CB Editions and most poetry publishing houses, his was a one-person band. Fifty years is a long busk.

Apart from Anvil, the two imprints I most value (beyond Carcanet) are the Welsh publishing house Seren, with its inspiring record of discovery and service, and Enitharmon, which I have followed since it was set up by Alan Clodd in 1967, and more attentively since, in 1987, it was taken over by Stephen Stuart-Smith.

Stephen wrote Clodd's obituary in the *Independent* in 2002. 'Alan Clodd was perhaps the last surviving example of a bookman in the nineteenth-century mould whose abilities and accomplishments extended into every area of the literary world – collecting, dealing, publishing and bibliographical research. He was no dilettante, however. His professionalism was absolute and was evinced when in 1967 he founded the Enitharmon Press, one of the most distinctive of English private presses, which he was to run single-handedly until his retirement from publishing in 1987. In an age of conglomerates he represented a vanishing breed of publishers whose care with the text and dedication to their authors was more important than the balance sheet. His insistence on quality in every area of book production was central to his operation, and in his dealings with authors he was gentlemanly, discreet and encouraging.'

Now, thirty years after Clodd's retirement, Stephen writes to me (29 January) that Enitharmon will continue in a different form, the change compelled by factors that anyone in the independent press sector knows all too well. 'This year, 2017, marks the fiftieth anniversary of Enitharmon Press. Although there is much to celebrate in the achievements of the past and the present, we are now entering a new phase in our history.' His 'our history' includes Peter Jay, Charles Boyle and all of us in the business. His no-nonsense analysis is bleak.

'Last weekend I was in touch with all my writers to explain the changes that are to take place in the next few months, and I wanted to let you know too, as I imagine some of them might come knocking on your door. The past six years have been more than usually challenging. In 2011, Enitharmon Press and 200 other Arts Council England clients lost their regular funding status, and since then we have been obliged to put in annual applications for funding from Grants for the Arts (GftA) to keep the show on the road. We've had an excellent run of success in each of the subsequent years, receiving more than we would have done if we'd remained a regularly funded organisation, but each year the process has become more competitive and time-consuming. GftA funding is now so oversubscribed that they are able to make awards to only 34% of applicants. Although ACE have been encouraging and rate Enitharmon as an organisation of outstanding artistic excellence, neither of our latest applications, in June and November 2016, was successful.'

No blame, Stephen insists, attaches to Arts Council England (ACE): it has a Solomonic task. Applicants to ACE know the challenges – some of them clarifying and constructive – that go to making a bid; they know the labour that application entails, and the spurns that patient merit takes.

'A more significant factor,' Stephen continues, 'is the dramatic downturn in trading conditions – the most difficult I have experienced in my thirty years as Director. Independent bookshops have all but disappeared, and with them the collegiate relationship between publishers and booksellers. Library suppliers, who in my first years at Enitharmon were a crucial sales outlet, have also dwindled in number and influence, as have the libraries themselves, bludgeoned by government cuts. But the most significant change has been the rise of the gargantuan bookshop chains and the likes of Amazon, whose highly selective choice of titles and bullying demands for higher and higher discounts have made our type of books (small print-runs of quality literature with high production standards) commercially unviable.'

There are too rising costs of materials and services, rents and rates, with Brexit knocking sterling for six. He does not mention the decline in poetry book-buying and collecting, or the ways in which the web quietly side-steps copyright and gives readers much of what they want gratis. But the 'conjunction of circumstances has reluctantly brought us to the point where we can no longer publish new titles. We have a further four titles to produce between now and June, and Lawrence Sail's monumental and magnificent anthology, *The Heart's Granary*, celebrating fifty years of Enitharmon Press (1967–2017), will be the final hurrah.'

Enitharmon is not walking away from its authors. It will keep faith with them, distributing and promoting their backlist and paying royalties. It makes these changes at the time of its choosing, at the peak of its reputation, 'with all our flags flying'. The gallery and the art books will continue to make their unique contribution. But its list of beautiful, editorially surprising and rewarding new poetry books will not grow. Another long-lived, irreplaceable organism turns into a gorgeous fossil before our eyes. Poetry readers owe Stephen a debt that, because editors are generally invisible, they are unlikely ever to pay.

Carcanet and *PN Review* have applied to the Arts Council for renewed funding for 2018–2022. 'We work on the principle that the reader completes the poet's work,' we declare, 'and that the growth of an informed, responsive readership is as crucial to poetry as the health of the critical culture surrounding us.' Those readers need to be active subscribers and book-buyers who know the importance of a strong independent sector in which market forces are not the *sine qua non*. In another country a market ideology leads towards the destruction of the National Endowment for the Arts, struck down by a tweet and a presidential decree. Here, it is still possible to hear Pound's injunction, 'Only what's been written against the market!'

News & Notes

'He is not dead but sleeping' · At the age of ten (AD 2007–2016) CB Editions seems to be over. Is it death or a restless sleep? The eponymous CB, Charles Boyle, sent out a self-obituary just as the old year ended. The metaphor he used was that of the one-man (he is sufficiently modern to call it 'one-person') band. He will now be in 'hobbyist' mode and resurrect at will, if something takes his fancy. 'A part of the fun has been proving – to myself as much as anyone – what can be done with little money and no funding. Extracurricular activities have included, in 2011, a London book fair for poetry presses (now an annual event) and a pop-up shop in Portobello Road for a week in 2013. Should I mention the gongs? CBe titles have won the McKitterick Prize, the Scott Moncrieff Translation Prize and the Aldeburgh First Collection Prize (three times), and have been shortlisted for the Goldsmiths Prize, the Guardian First Book Award, the Forward main prize (twice) and the Forward first collection Prize (four times) and more.' It seems unlikely that this is the last or even the penultimate word: CB Editions predicted its demise once before, and survived. Even now, CB admits there are possible books in the works, but fewer of them, less of him. It is regrettable to be on the threshold of spring without the promise of a continuing supply of his handsome, unexpected, invariably excellent books. 'For the record: 57 titles, rough count. Heinz Means Beans. Placed in a pile on the floor, the total run of these books comes to around 64 cm, just over 2 feet, not much above my knees. Around 30 authors. [...] Three of the authors have died since I published their books, one at the age of 37. The oldest author on the list is 95. I have stood in line at the post office 1,147 times.'

John Montague · contributed by MARY O'MALLEY · John Montague, who died in Nice on 10 December 2016, was one of Ireland's finest poets. Born in Brooklyn, New York, in 1929, he was sent to be reared by an aunt in Garvaghy, Co Tyrone. Those early years were to provide the subject and locus of his most celebrated work.

He went south to attend University College Dublin, and a Fulbright scholarship took him to Yale in 1953. He subsequently spent time in Iowa and Berkeley, where he met his first wife, Madeleine de Brauer, and came under the influence of the American poets including John Berryman and Hayden Carruth.

By the time he joined the English Department at University College Cork, he had published several books, including *Tides* and *Poisoned Lands*. Some of those books were published by Liam Miller of Dolmen Press, also a formative influence on Thomas Kinsella, whom Montague held in high regard. He lived many years in Cork with his second wife, Evelyn Robson, and his two daughters, Oonagh and Sybil.

The Rough Field came out in 1972, an extended sequence about Northern Ireland which took its name and much of its inspiration from the townland of Garvaghy. It perturbed some and excited many, with its eloquent interrogation of received truths. It succeeded in doing what Montague himself would later suggest was the essence of the poet's work: turning psychic defeats into victories on the page.

Montague collaborated with the composer Sean O'Riada and was a involved in setting up Claddagh Records, which recorded poets and musicians and released a number of recordings of Montague himself, including a reading at the Roundhouse in London with The Chieftains, the band which took its name from Montague's poem 'Death of a Chieftain'.

In the 1960s he started to spend time in France, reporting from Paris for the *Irish Times*. He was a friend of Samuel Beckett, to whom he referred as 'the Garbo of Irish letters', and they continued to meet until Beckett's death. He settled in Nice with his third wife, Elizabeth Wassell, in the mid-1990s, coming back to Ireland every summer and when occasion demanded.

In all, John Montague published more than thirty books of poems, essays and short stories, including most notably *The Great Cloak*, *The Dead Kingdom*, *Mount Eagle* and *Time in Armagh*. His *Collected Poems* was published in 1995 and a *New and Collected* in 2012. He published three volumes of memoirs, and *The Pear is Ripe*, a volume of essays. *Second Childhood*, a posthumous collection of poems, will be published later this year.

From *The Rough Field* to the late, masterly *Border Sick Call* which closes the first edition of his *Collected Poems*, Montague has given voice to Northern Ireland in collection after collection, in poems of political weight and literary merit that have yet to gain full recognition. *Border Sick Call*, about an epic border journey with his brother, a doctor, repeats the motif of circling to be found throughout his work in a meditation on death that is healing, because shared: '...When we stride again on the road / there is a bright crop of stars / the high, clear stars of winter...'

Marked by a riven sense of place and 'forked tongue', as steeped in the song and tradition of Tyrone and South Armagh as he was in French literature, Montague was also enlivened by the American poets who were his contemporaries. He became a Chevalier de la légion d'honneur in 2010 and held the first post as Ireland Professor of Poetry.

He was a poet, to quote his own words from his introduction to the 1974 *Faber Book of Irish Verse*, 'balanced between the pastoral and atomic age' and continued working until the end, giving a series of electrifying readings in recent years.

John Berger · Art critic, essayist and novelist: those are the main sobriquets applied to John Berger, who died on 2 January 2017, in the obituaries. That he also wrote poems, and that those poems set out to challenge conventional readers much as his art criticism challenged conventional viewers, was not much mentioned. The poems were scattered, and not collected in English until 2014 when Smokestack Books, with its mission of 'championing poets who are unfashionable, radical, left-field and working a long way from the metropolitan centres of cultural authority', published a *Collected Poems*.

We knew he read poetry: he reviewed Nicki Jackowska's *New and Selected Poems* in PNR 133, admiring the speed and narrative directness of the writing. 'All the stories are the invention of the voice telling them, and therein lies their marvelous and very contemporary poetry.' Not a single voice, but the voice each story requires.

Years ago – some time in the 1980s – at the Mauritshaus in The Hague I had gone to see Vermeer's *View of Delft*. I stood before the painting, thinking of Bergotte and Proust and how much this painting drew out of the fictional character and the living writer. A man, woman and child came into the room. The child was bored and threw himself backwards over a leather bench in the middle of the room. The man began to explain the painting to the woman. He said that Proust admired it because if you focused at any point on the canvas, and not just the 'petit pan du mur jaune', the whole picture composed around that point, whether it was a corner, a window, a patch of water, a single brick – as in *Á la recherché du temps perdu*, where any point in the action is the focal point, and the narrative re-configures itself around that point, incident, event. The man was strikingly familiar. 'Are you John Berger?' It was.

His poem 'A View from Delft' (the preposition inverted) is also vaguely dated '1980s'. It exemplifies his ways of seeing and seeing with, his sense of inherences, and his deep love of an historical and a living person, the one being a condition for the other.

In that town,
across the water
where all has been seen
and the bricks are cherished like sparrows,
in that town like a letter from home
read again and again in a port,
in that town with its library of tiles
and its addresses recalled by Johannes Vermeer
who died in debt,
in that town across the water
where the dead take the census
and there are no vacant rooms
for his gaze occupies them all,
where the sky is waiting
to have news of a birth,
in that town which pours from the eyes
of those who left it,
there
between two chimes of the morning,
when fish are sold in the square
and the maps on the walls
show the depth of the sea,
in that town
I am preparing for your arrival.

In 1976 he looked at the same painting in prose, in 'Drawn to that Moment' (reprinted in *Berger on Drawing*, 2005). 'The painted moment has remained (almost) unchanged for three centuries. The reflections in the water have not moved. Yet this painted moment, as we look at it, has a plenitude of actuality that we experience only rarely in life. We experience everything we see in the painting as *absolutely* momentary. At the same time the experience is repeatable the next day or in ten years. It would be naïve to suppose that this has to do with accuracy: Delft at any given moment never looked like this painting. It has to do with the density per square millimetre of Vermeer's looking, with the density per square millimetre of assembled moments.'

David Meltzer · The prolific Beat poet and musician David Meltzer died on the last day of 2016 at the age of seventy-nine. New York-born, Meltzer was associated with the Beats from his early twenties, appearing in Beat anthologies and settling at last in the San Francisco Bay area, where many of the Beats made their homes.

His work was featured in Allen Ginsberg's and John Ashbery's *The New American Poetry 1945–1960*. He published prose and poetry. A retrospective of his verse, *David's Copy: The Selected Poems of David Meltzer*, was published by Penguin in 2005. Lawrence Ferlinghetti admired him and published his work with City Lights, and Black Sparrow produced handsome editions of his work.

As well as being a poet, jazz musician (song-writer and guitarist) and musical collaborator, he wrote prose books, appeared on television and radio. He taight at the New College of California and served on the board of the Before Columbus Foundation devoted to multicultural writing.

Spring Couplet · Controversy flared in Taiwan (reported in *The China Post*, 1 February) when President Tsai Ing-wen's contribution to the annual spring couplet ceremony was criticized for being 'incorrect'. Her defenders preferred to call her structuring 'unusual'. The head of the National Museum of Taiwanese Literature applauded the President's attempt, increasing awareness of Taiwan's literary culture, but it wouldn't quite do as a spring couplet: 'The president's spring couplets could probably count as two lines of new year greetings, but couplets? Not so much.' A number of rules constrain the spring couplet in terms of number of characters per line, the lexical category of each character in relation to their corresponding characters, and the tone patterns: one line must reverse the tone pattern of the other. The President rooted her couplet in one by Lai He, the 'father of modern Taiwanese literature'. Her office expressed its respect for diverse opinions and wished everyone a happy spring.

Pablo Larraín's *Neruda* · contributed by ADAM FEINSTEIN · Anyone seeking the truth about the life of Chile's great Nobel Prize-winning poet Pablo Neruda should look elsewhere than Pablo Larraín's latest film. And Larraín himself would have it no other way. He knows the facts. He's read the books on Neruda (including my biography). He says he is an admirer of realistic filmmakers like Mike Leigh. 'But I can't do that. For me, cinema is related to the old magicians, the illusionists.'

Neruda does indeed turn out to be an 'anti-biopic'. It is set in Santiago in 1948, at the height of the Cold War. This was an extraordinary period of Neruda's life, one which the poet himself called 'a year of blind rats'. Already renowned for his *Twenty Love Poems and a Song of Despair*, he stood up in the Senate (where he represented the Communist Party) and condemned Chile's President, Gabriel González Videla, for turning against the party which had helped to bring him to power and for behaving as thuggishly and fascistically as Franco in Spain. (Neruda had witnessed Franco's brutality, and the murder of his friend and fellow poet Federico García Lorca, while Chilean consul in Madrid in 1936.) For his courageous outspokenness in Santiago in 1948, Neruda was deprived of his parliamentary immunity and forced into hiding, rushed from one safe house to another, sometimes in the middle of the night, to avoid being captured and taken to the concentration camp at Pisagua, in the northern Atacama desert (where the commandant was a certain Augusto Pinochet). He eventually escaped across the Andes on horseback into Argentina and made his way to Europe using the passport of his fellow writer, the Guatemalan novelist Miguel Ángel Asturias.

This would have made a thrilling movie. Instead, Larraín chooses to subvert reality. He tells the story from the perspective of the fedora-sporting police inspector Óscar Peluchonneau (played here with admirable intensity and poignancy by Gael García Bernal), who is leading the hunt for Neruda. Most critics have maintained that Peluchonneau is an imaginary figure. Not so. He really existed, although not as he appears here. Indeed, his son, Jorge Peluchonneau Cádiz, told the BBC that he could not understand why the filmmakers chose to use his name, since his father emerges unrecognisable. After it is decided that Neruda must flee Chile, the poet (interpreted impressively by Luis Gnecco, all corpulence and knowingness) exclaims: 'I'm not going to hide under the bed. This has to become a wild hunt!' And wild it certainly becomes. Both he and his pursuer crave fame. Both want to be remembered – one as a poet, the other for capturing a poet. But both come reluctantly to realise, especially in the increasingly elegiac second half of the film, that they are, in some way, validating each other.

Larraín sought a Borgesian structure: 'I realised it could work as a meta-fictional labyrinth where characters are creating other characters. Each needs the other in order to exist. All these characters – Neruda, Óscar the detective, the narrator who narrates himself into the story – all of them are creating each other because they need each other to tell the story. The film is about storytelling and how we need to tell stories in order to survive life.'

His aim was, indeed, to approach the poet through the 'arbitrariness of fiction'. But the film, the director insists, also has elements of *film noir*, a cat-and-mouse chase thriller, a road movie, a western and a black comedy. Neruda, himself a life-long lover of detective novels, would at least have enjoyed the suspense. However, Larraín's film also indulges in Buñuelesque surrealism, which Neruda himself had rejected at this time in his life. Indeed, the film's opening scene could come straight out of Buñuel: Neruda is seen pissing in the chamber of the Santiago Senate, which mysteriously doubles as an opulent urinal. Elsewhere, Larraín deliberately injects Hitchcockian artifice: for example, the use of conspicuous back-projection as Peluchonneau is driving his car.

Larraín told one interviewer: 'I'm Chilean. Neruda is in the water, in the earth, in the trees [...] This is a movie about the Neruda cosmos.' But for all Neruda's genuine passion for life, the Rabelaisian excesses in the film have a sleaziness that his friends would not have recognised. Neruda's second wife Delia del Carril (portrayed affectionately by Mercedes Morán) shared many of Neruda's most difficult moments in hiding. You would not know, however, from this film – and from the scornful way Neruda occasionally talks to her – that Delia was a talented painter and an enormously cultured woman whom he adored, who had been instrumental in firing his political commitment (during the Spanish Civil War) and who was his most astute and attentive literary critic.

We should not be surprised by Larraín's approach. The forty-year-old director has never aimed for straightforward docudrama. His Oscar-nominated 2012 film, *No*, based on a Chilean political advertising campaign during the Pinochet dictatorship in the 1980s, was shot with forty-year-old technology to make it look like a TV commercial from that era. A specific filmic influence on Larraín was Maurice Pialat's 1991 movie *Van Gogh*: 'Pialat used the paintings as a mirror. That's how I approached Neruda. We used Neruda's poetry to create the structure. I insisted that we would get the audience to realise that we are playing with the characters. Nothing is entirely serious. It is more based on poetry than anything else. Neruda's poetry was a virus that infected us all.'

Those who know little of Neruda's life will enjoy the imaginative and provocative playfulness of Larraín's direction and the fine performances of Gnecco, García Bernal and Morán. The screenplay, by Guillermo Calderón, certainly has its moments, for all its detachment from historical veracity. (Peluchonneau remarks, at one point, that poets 'tend to think that the world is something they imagined', and as he trudges through the snow on the trail of his prey, he begins to fear, sadly, that he himself may be no more than a figment of Neruda's invention.) The cinematography of Sergio Armstrong (Larraín's regular photographer), with its use of *chiaroscuro* and faded colours, is sumptuous.

Nevertheless, Larraín makes too many sacrifices in his relentless determination to flee the facts. He deprives his audience of some astonishingly rich (and cinematic) moments. The idea that Neruda could walk freely down a street while a fugitive from justice, as he does in this film, is laughable. In his memoirs, he actually described gazing out longingly at a shoe shop from his cramped hiding place in Valparaíso. What a touching shot that would have made! Larraín could also have shown us the profoundly moving incident when Neruda ended up hiding on the estate of the right-wing mill-owner Pepe Rodríguez, a friend of President González Videla, who would have been expected to hand over Neruda immediately to the authorities. Instead, Rodríguez was utterly delighted to meet Chile's greatest poet and urged his workers to ensure Neruda escaped. Poetry breaking down political barriers. Poetry as a force for good. But it's not in the movie.

The struggle between freedom and tyranny is a central theme of the film. So it is a pity that Larraín fails to highlight one of the great paradoxes in twentieth-century literature. While Neruda was living in extremely confined spaces, he wrote much of his most expansive book, *Canto General*, with its twin themes of betrayal: the personal betrayal by President González Videla and the savage betrayal of pre-Columbian civilisation by the Spanish Conquistadors. Instead, Larraín shows us a Neruda in bordellos repeatedly reciting the famous Poem Twenty from the *Twenty Love Poems and a Song of Despair*, written more than two decades earlier in 1924. Of course, Larraín is playing with the lability of time here. That is his prerogative. (His other new release, the much-lauded English-language *Jackie*, starring Natalie Portman as Jacqueline Kennedy after the assassination of her husband, also plays around with time.) But if Larraín genuinely believes, as he has stated, in the transformative power of art, why not have Neruda read the wonderfully evocative and tender poem from *Canto General*, 'The Fugitive,' in which Neruda reveals himself not as the 'rock star' celebrity but as the humanist poet, expressing gratitude to the strangers who took him in during this year underground?

From the Archive
Issue 34, November–December 1983

RACHEL HADAS

From a contribution of two poems, the other titled 'Taking the Train Home from Maine'. Fellow contributors to this issue include Bill Manhire, Donald Davie, Idris Parry, Nicolas Tredell, Alison Brackenbury, and Robert Pinsky.

WINTER DAY AND EVENING

The biggest sun on one side
and on the other the new moon
distant in memory like those breasts.

SEFERIS, 'Summer Solstice'

Instead of climbing as we'd planned
into the mountain foothills,
we foundered at the first steep slope
and lost ourselves in snow.

Later it cleared but stayed too cold to thaw.
We drove through redbrown rocks
still crosshatched in hollows
with clinging scribbles of ice.

Then evening: brazen dazzle.
As we headed home by way of the mesa,
sun and moon pulled the world taut between them.
How can anyone not take these as visitations?

The horizontal valley
blossoms: mesa
great agate rink
glowing garnet-dark.

What plucks silkily
at the cat's cradle
luminous and dim
strung over the sky?

Waxing and waning
will x out the balance.
Sphere against sphere:
I meet my sister's eye.

Madwoman: What Compelled You

Vahni Capildeo

RED IS THE COLOUR of *Madwoman*'s cover. It is as if darkness has menstruated on to a cloth of blood or rectangle of glass: a textured black blotch on the shiny red has edges like a clot or stain on laundry or a scientist's slide. The title word is in a huge font, split into three: MAD WO MAN, like a stepped line, like a set of imperfectly flipped or reflected forms, like a ruination of the quintessential masculine poet Ted Hughes's title *Wodwo*, like an Oulipian word-transformation by letter-substitution leading from sanity through grief to gender. The intense shades and shapes of Pamela MacKay's cover art for Shara McCallum's 2017 collection from Peepal Tree Press make holding the book feel like drenching one's hands: staunching a wound, operating on a specimen, sharing in a crime scene. The visual impression is excessive, powerful, patchy, unbalanced, fabricated: adjectives that, like 'mad', belong to the vocabulary, mindset and structures that continue to silence or invalidate women, whether the demonised Creole Bertha Rochester of Charlotte Brontë's fiction and Jean Rhys's nightmare-as-memoir, or the women whom juries consider unreliable merely because of their culturally inflected body language, as reported and analysed in Helena Kennedy's polemic about the law, *Eve Was Framed: Women and British Justice*.

Madwoman's fifty-four poems have titles that speak to each other, like the echo chamber of a 'mad' – or remembering – mind. Memory, and medical labels, both make and unmake, and McCallum is deft and insistent in never letting the text rest too long on any one sense; the epigraph, from Lisel Mueller, nominates 'memory' as the only understandable 'after-life', but the first poem, a reworking after Hadrian, assures the 'little soul' that what once compelled her 'is no more'. 'Madwoman as Salome' is answered, far across the book, by 'Salome to Madwoman'; this also recalls the epistolary form popular in early novels of the feminine sensibility (the psyche's drag of *Clarissa*), and the communication by letter that by the twentieth century had become naturalised as part of the way of thinking of the voices of home, whether one was at home or abroad. 'Madwoman as Rasta Medusa' is followed by 'Oh Abuse', and the sounds run together, making an extra poem out of the liquidity of the contents list. Time runs wayward: a 'Coda' uncurls less than halfway through the volume, while an 'Ode to the Apple' features long after a number of religious, mythological, and modern figures have made their appearance in story and parable, study and fable, news and blues. However, linear chronology is only an intermittent interest of these linguistically neat and deadly texts: they turn repeatedly on spoiled or poisonous Edens; their genesis, and the exile's nostalgia for them; on recollection, looking, and not-looking. The manchineel poem is a poison-apple poem, where 'the children' survive contact with the 'skin-blistering sap' of *Hippomane mancinella*, the all too real tree whose shiny leaves

and sweet fruit literally exhale and exude toxicity. The apple poem is a pomegranate poem and a rose poem. A merciful father, not a wrathful godhead, slices a fruit for his daughter:

Oh, but that was some time ago,
and I've since grown a taste for tart, for bitter
lacing every sweet. And you

could never deliver the kind of freedom
I've long been after – to have no need
to make an Eden of this world, or any other.

('Ode to the Apple', p. 57)

'You' and 'I' stand just four poems apart. 'You' is a relative of ghazal, landay, and Old Hollywood crooner song – and it is all about 'me':

You bring out the ragged in me.
The razor-edged, cellophane, jagged in me.
[...]
You bring out the rivers in me.
And the seas and the oceans eroding in me.

You bring out the groveller in me.
The beggar, deal-maker, tightrope-walker in me.

(p. 62)

'You' is akin to 'She' in its all-singing, all-dancing, postlapsarian jag:

She could sing a lesson in a yardstick
She could sing the duppy out of night
She could sing the shoeless out of homesick
She could sing a wrong out of a right

(p. 45)

'I' (page 67) announces itself somewhat academically, as *'fragments and definitions'*. 'I' is the first letter of 'Invention', the title of the next poem, which concludes: '*Shara*, you are the most fleeting of my inventions.'

Personally, I find the book's exploration of memory and the continual re-invention of self in relation to trauma, one of its bravest and most engaging aspects: the replays, the soundscape of lyric description interrupted by verbal aggressions, the splitting of sense of self from body, body as soulcase, the untimely or out-of-time return of things past. Central to the narrative of self (the book is not a 'narrative', nor even a diagnostic manual of selves) is an experience of sexual assault. 'Running' demonstrates how subsequent fear becomes concretised and repetitive, and an assailant, though gone, continues to live in light effects and the passage of time that would otherwise be ordinary or even pastoral:

not chancing a glance behind to see the sun
draining the sky of colour, the sun slung low on the horizon

at this hour, this hour reprising every twilight
in you, in you every falling again into night.

'Abuse' occasionally answers the name of 'you' in
this work.

    'Ten Things You Might Like to Know about
Madwoman' consists of seventeen sections, some
of which label themselves as subsections, 8b and
5c between 8 and 9. Fey, roundabout, whimsical:
these are the sweeter inflections of the 'madwoman'
stereotype, yet it is possible to find pleasure, too,
in dancing with a text that is so knowing about its
disorderliness, so perfectly skilled in syncopating
its forms just beyond the expected beat or margin.
It reminds me of seeing McCallum herself dancing
one evening, with discomfiting ecstasy, her stint of
literary duties over for the week, her green eyes and
green dress flashing, light pouring over her sweat
pores until she danced like her own sea. The final,
unusually long poem, 'Madwoman Apocrypha', plays
with spacing, italicisation, and a question-and-
answer format, but most importantly it plays with
justifications in more than the printer's sense of the
term. The speaker who poses each question marked
as 'Q', and pursues an intrusive, prosy, biographical
interrogation which seeks to pin down the poet in
the work, is not the only questioner. Another voice,
italicised, keeps floating in with an alternating, dou-
ble refrain: *When comes the night that made you?* and
When comes the night of your unmaking? The moment
of unmaking, or where the words come to a stop, is
in the rewind where a child has acquired language,
applies 'bird' as word to frosted glass thing, and
asks: '*Granny, when yu dead I can have these birds?*'
This is the differentiation of self from ancestress,
and it is also the crystallisation of elegy (there has
been death in the taken-from-life stories) into the
impossible continuation of a conversation via a
question that has had its response, and now remains
poised as if waiting for another.

Letter from Paris

Jennie Feldman

As the wind picked up, a dozen scattered
sailing boats tilted and gathered speed across the
pea-green water. One with a Union Jack traced a
wide arc around others flying the flags of France,
the Netherlands, Japan; seconds later it was chafing
against the stone wall and a small boy raced past me
to prod it back into action.

    On my previous visit to the Jardin du Luxembourg,
the model boats for hire had still sported numbers
for you to choose from. The wide octagonal pool
was its own world. With the switch to national flags,
the scene now suggests either inconsequential
Olympic rivalry or (as I couldn't help seeing it) a
mad, if graceful, enactment of current affairs. When
a German-flagged craft overtakes another – with,
inevitably, a Greek flag – and almost collides with
an Italian one, windblown child's play comes gid-
dily close to political realities. At the boat-hire stall
someone asked if the Union Jack would now have
to go – a favourite quip, the good-humoured young
man in charge told me. Luckily a pirate skiff with
black sails and a skull-and-crossbones is there to
reinforce the imaginative aspect (and the childish
fancy that piracy is confined to fiction), as well as
three unflappable Jemima Puddle-Ducks cruising
near the fountain at the pool's dead centre.

    I was in Paris for the launch of a new anthology
of poems from some sixty different nationalities
and languages. As the audience gathered under the
trees outside Shakespeare and Company bookshop,
small groups of soldiers – a new feature on the city's
streets – patrolled the adjacent Quai de Montebello
and Petit Pont. Soon Notre Dame, surprisingly close,
would light up against the night. *Centres of Cataclysm*,
a selection celebrating fifty years of *Modern Poetry in
Translation*, addresses themes of 'war, oppression,
revolution, hope and survival'. Ted Hughes
co-founded the magazine with Daniel Weissbort in
1965 at the height of the Cold War. In their introduc-
tion to the first issue, cited during the evening, they
said that of all the material reaching them 'the most
insistent' came from Eastern Europe – poems by Cze-
slaw Miłosz, Vasko Popa and Miroslav Holub, among
others – that region having been 'at the centre of cat-
aclysm'. In keeping with the early description of MPT
as 'an airport for incoming translations', the event by
the Seine featured arrivals from Burmese, German,
Greek, Italian, Macedonian, Hebrew and French.

    Well known for his advocacy of poetry – 'its natural
sympathy for plurality of being' – and the humanising
role of literary translation, David Constantine, the
anthology's co-editor (with Helen Constantine and
Sasha Dugdale) struck an altered, urgent note when he
took the microphone. Britain's recent 'criminal folly'
had made him realise, he admitted wryly, that for fifty
percent of his countrymen, all that he had said and
done, 'the whole thing I've given my life to', meant
absolutely nothing. Going out and winning people
over was unlikely. His conclusion? 'We need to keep
talking to one another, to fortify one another', widen-
ing the contacts – 'that's the whole business, really.'

    The readings concluded with a poem by Apol-
linaire to his beloved, written in the trenches
'between the whizzbangs and the casseroles'. Behind
us, occasional sirens and car horns became, like any
good soundtrack, complicit in the occasion rather
than obtrusive. Poetry's transcendent, universal
charge – not least in translation – stood out with
particular poignancy that evening: earlier in the day
a priest had been murdered in Normandy by Moslem
fanatics, the shock of it still palpable.

    Over the dinner afterwards, Fergal Keane, a guest

reader at the launch, quoted by heart James Joyce's Stephen Dedalus: 'When the soul of a man is born in this country there are nets flung at it to hold it back from flight. You talk to me of nationality, language, religion. I shall try to fly by those nets.' Around the table there was talk of childhood, how we inhabit it still; for at least two poets, from Iraq and Macedonia, it was the true homeland. Our gathering inevitably brought to mind the role of Paris in the last century as a locus of exile; Shakespeare and Company stands as a vestige of that era.

Saint-Germain, a couple of streets away, is the setting for a dreamy encounter between Jacques Réda – one of the poets I have translated in the anthology – and the subject of his new book, Jean de La Fontaine. At one of the *quartier*'s cafés I began reading the copy Réda had given me. The fabulist, resplendent in wig and buckled shoes, steps into view at the opening of *La Fontaine*, part of a new series in which a French writer focuses on a favourite classical author. Réda's selection for the book includes 'Les Lunettes' – new to me, its bawdiness elegantly oblique – as well as some of the better-known *contes* and fables. One of these, 'Le Lion amoureux', would feature – 'materialise', you might say – in the museum I was about to visit.

When you enter the Musée Nissim de Camondo, an impressive mansion overlooking Parc Monceau, the audio guide announces that this is a private residence 'built for the family of Moïse de Camondo and his children, Nissim and Béatrice'. By the end of my visit, I was struck less by Moïse's grand collection of eighteenth-century furniture and *objets d'art* – a lifelong project that he bequeathed to the State before his death in 1935 – than by the fate of his children, overtaken by the century's two major cataclysms, to adopt the MPT term. In a film about the family shown in a small upper room, we learn that Nissim, after whom his grieving father named the place, had been killed (*mort glorieuse*) in aerial combat in World War I. His sister Béatrice felt no personal danger when the Germans occupied Paris – she was a respected society figure and her father had given the State this house and its contents; his cousin had established the Louvre's Impressionist collection. Béatrice, her husband and their two children were arrested and sent on two separate transports, in 1942 and 1943, to Auschwitz. The film concludes: the family is now extinguished (*est désormais éteinte*). Stunned by this, I had not left my place when the screening recommenced. The story of the Camondos – who had fled the persecution of Jews in fifteenth-century Spain, eventually becoming bankers and reformist philanthropists in Ottoman Turkey before migrating to France – suggested a reprise of the MPT anthology's stated themes, but in reverse order: survival, hope, revolution, oppression, war.

Before descending the grand staircase (trodden by Marcel Proust, a guest at the glittering social gatherings), I glanced into the study with its six large tapestries illustrating fables by La Fontaine – and there he was, the naïve, lovelorn lion who had forfeited teeth and claws to win the shepherdess, gasping his last as he is set upon outside her house.

'*Comment vivre avec la peur?*' asked a headline I spotted in someone's magazine on the bus back to Saint-Germain. The question of how to live with fear had come up several times in conversations with Parisian friends; it was in the air. At one point a small girl hopped off the bus at the wrong stop and her mother screamed in panic '*Non, non! Imbécile!*', dissolving into tears as the bewildered child hopped back on again. People nodded and murmured sympathetically to calm the woman, but once the two had left there was a general tut-tutting over her hysteria. One had to keep self-control these days, *quand même*.

As we crossed the Seine a fellow passenger commented on the plague of rats – '*Quelle horreur!*' – flushed above ground by the river's recent flooding. There came to mind one of the fables in Réda's book, 'Le Chat et un vieux rat', in which 'the Alexander of cats / the Attila, the scourge of rats' is outwitted by a cautious, savvy old-timer. I had seen a few of his sort in the bushes near the Petit Pont.

Looking for Lorca

TREVOR BARNETT

I HAVE WALKED DOWN the road on which Lorca was murdered more times than I care to remember. It takes only an hour – what an hour! – to travel from the outskirts of one *whitewash-and-myrtle* Andalusian village to another, from Víznar to Alfacar, and to take in some of the finest views of the mustardy-gold plains and the foothills to the north-east of Granada lined with pines. Following the eleventh-century irrigation channel – aqueduct, ditch, tunnel; *water and shade, shade and water* – the road, serpentine and clean of *bloodstains made by the sun or the moon*, takes a rest at each bend as the traveller listens to the gathering silences of the *sierra*. Above, the cross that marks the highest peak – *and halfway down the road they took him, one on each arm.*

The near-silence of a village like Víznar, one of thousands of villages of its kind across Spain, is part of its charm. Only those who have slept a siesta on a balcony giving onto its square can say, I now know what it is to feel bliss. Look up at the Neoclassical facade of the Church of Saint Pilar, and over there to see the Italianate gardens of the palace: fading murals of Don Quixote can be glimpsed through the cracks in those shutters. Lower your lips to the fountain water which even in the August heat maintains the cool taste of earth. Here, in the midsummer, midday sun, try to imagine anything other than the capacity of humankind for poetry and beauty – you will not succeed.

But I don't want to see it. The blood in the sand. I don't want to see that the palace was built with State funds given to the Bishop of Cuzco for his role in suppressing an uprising. I don't want to see that those gardens were patrolled by armed guards when the palace was the barracks in the war, when all these houses were billets. At night they rumbled through this square in their trucks. I don't want to hear what Víznar's children heard as they lay in their beds wondering what could be making such an ungodly noise at such an hour. Get away from the window, Antonio, they'll see the light. *Dios mío, Dios mío*. This square was only a gunshot's distance from over 1,300 hurried graves.

Víznar is, of course, not the only place in the world with bloodstains on the cobbles. Most heritage sites and postcard-sized cityscapes contain their share. A military HQ in one century becomes a luxury hotel in the next. When we pose in front of the Alhambra and smile under its impossibly romantic charm, we can forget what History barely hides from us. For who wants to think of garrotings and the cruel dawn chorus of the execution squad when eating their ham sandwich? *I came to this world with eyes and I leave it without them*. Yet some stories from the past petrify with time, like Lorca's death; as they turn to stone they change the way we read them. Lorca: poet, martyr, soothsayer. Now every line of his poetry seems to lead to his grave.

Lorca's grave. It could be here in this patch of scorched grass. Imagine what this circling buzzard has seen in this plot. A field is a field is a field, but we do not all take in the view with the same feeling of concordance between the natural world and the mind. A developer arrives and sees six extra digits in his bank account; the archaeologist sees her photo under the headline 'Roman Hoard Discovery'; the poet, a poem; and a researcher on Lorca's final resting place sees Lorca's final resting place. All these years after his death they still don't know where he is. The next village, Alfacar, has built a Federico García Lorca park near the supposed site which is now included as part of a ghoulish tour of 'Lorca's final hours in Granada'. Is this what we come for with our digital cameras and guidebooks? Is this why we read Lorca?

Over the years I have taken many photos on this same road, *el camino de la fuente*, or as Google Maps knows it, the GR3101. Giorgos (whatever happened to Giorgos?), my future wife and her friend pose in one just before the sky melts from honey to tiger to clay. Our faces are grinning with the full burst of youth even though we would not see Giorgos again, even though we would soon be old, even though we were walking towards the place where Lorca was murdered, and Joaquín was murdered, and Dióscoro, and Paco. Then we married in Víznar years later and linked arms with our family for that photo in front of the same church that Lorca would have seen from the back of that truck. He knew where he was then. *Oh, the grief of the hidden riverbed and the far-away morning*. I think I recall my wife's grandmother telling me once about the time Lorca come to her family's house in Víznar for afternoon tea. Did she not say how he sat, on that terrace, with his legs crossed, talking animatedly about books and plays as he looked out at the early snows on the Sierra Nevada? *You can see from the railings, on the mountain, mountain, mountain…*

I remember in my first year in Spain that moonlit walk on this road on 18th August – the date they shot Lorca, our son's birthday, my wife's saint's day. Every year in Víznar the local gypsies commemorate Lorca's death with a flamenco tribute. We walked with the other villagers down the road towards the light on the hillside. That was the house where H. died, down there was the old mill, this plot was almost bought by T., but D. refused to sell it because of what his granddad did in the war. That was where Lorca is buried, one said. Over there, on that bend. The others nodded in shame that it was here, not far from their tranquil village, that Lorca was murdered. *The moon bought paintings from death*. On the way home a mountain goat followed us like a memory, keeping about twenty paces behind, waiting for us to feed it or chase it back, its horns floating in the darkness.

Ten years after our wedding we are in Víznar again, walking up the same road. It is 80 years since Lorca was shot here. Some keep searching for him; others know better. The crickets let their onomatopoeias linger; *the frog song turns the irrigation channel into an enchanted, out of tune syringe*. The breeze moves across the tops of the *meditating pines*: it knows no poetry, no memories, no Lorca. Back in the village square the cobbles and shutters echo the fountain's restless return.

LETTERS   JOSHUA WEINER WRITES:

I was pleased to read Andrew Latimer's essay 'Poetry for the Future: Thom Gunn and the Legacy of Poetry' [*PNR* 233], especially because the poem in question, 'Misanthropos', had such an important role to play in the development of Gunn's thinking about poetic form and his own ambitions for what poetry could do, or should at least try to do. The implications very much concern poetry's future, as Latimer boldly announces. Readers who are interested in a longer consideration of what the archive reveals about that poem might find my essay on it useful – it can be found in *At the Barriers: On the Poetry of Thom Gunn* (Chicago, 2009), the book of essays by various hands that launched the web exhibition cited in Latimer's fine essay.

Letter from Wales

Sam Adams

I BECAME A MEMBER of the Folio Society in the late 1950s, when you signed up to purchase a minimum of four volumes from the annual list and received a bonus book into the bargain. Charles Ede, who (with Christopher Sandford and Alan Bott) launched the society in 1947, when the book trade was still in austerity mode, must have had in mind people like me. Inspired by the sumptuous library of Professor Gwyn Jones at Aberystwyth, which I viewed with awe whenever I dared raise my eyes from *Beowulf*, I wanted a shelf of fine-looking spines to call my own. I relished every Folio Society classic I received, and the free gifts, often profusely illustrated essays on historical themes, were equally desirable. On the basis of what had become, after a shaky start, a commercially successful venture, in 1960 Charles Ede started Collectors' Corner as a branch of the Society. You applied, via your membership, to receive catalogues of original prints, drawings and water-colours, antiquities, manuscripts, early maps, rare books and so on. I had no idea that it was possible to buy genuine art and historical objects, many of surpassing interest and beauty, over the counter, or at least by Royal Mail (postage and packing free!). I was a little slow off the mark, but by 1966 was certainly on the mailing list. Many of the catalogues I received have disappeared over the years, but I still have a bundle of them, starting with number XXXIX, which I look over from time to time, my interest tinged with regret. With a modest income from teaching, and family commitments, my purchases were from the lower end of the price range, and carefully thought over at that. They include a North Wales landscape by William Payne, an engraving of sheep by Aristide Maillol for Vergil's *Georgics*, and a portfolio of 'Leaves from Famous European Books' (among them, the *Nuremberg Chronicle*, the second Folio Shakespeare, an exquisite specimen of early Roman lettering from an incunable by Sweynheim and Pannartz), for which I was allowed, by Charles Ede himself, to pay in three or four monthly instalments of five pounds. Five pounds seems to have been about the limit I set myself. For those with deeper pockets there were treasures indeed: in May 1970 you might have bought three very desirable signed prints, by Picasso, Vlamink and Van Dongen, for less than a thousand pounds.

Collectors' Corner was later renamed Folio Fine Art, but the catalogues continued as enthralling as ever and to receive my rapt attention. Among the items that fell most frequently within my reach were single leaves from 'western and oriental manuscripts'. I acquired a dozen or more, from the fourteenth and fifteenth centuries in the main. Framed, they deck our walls; their elegant lettering, intricate tracery and gold embellishment draw the eye and fill the mind with a sense of history. I could never afford one that incor-porated a miniature but they were to be had. In that same May 1970 catalogue mentioned above there was a leaf on vellum 'from a Book of Hours written and

illuminated not after 1350 in Lincolnshire' on which a 'large initial D for the opening of Lauds shows the risen Christ'. Thanks to the internet, I know where that 'East-Anglian miniature' went: to the British Library, its Folio Fine Art provenance duly noted. I learned from the same source that Christopher de Hamel examined another leaf from the same Book of Hours at the Lilly Library, Indiana University, Bloom-ington, and wrote it up in *Gilding the Lilly* (2010).

De Hamel's *Meetings with Remarkable Manuscripts* (Allen Lane, 2016) is a delight – such lovingly detailed descriptions of manuscripts, the boxes in which they are stored, and the various repositories of knowledge where they are now held. It is a wonder of scholarly exactitude and clarity. In the chapter headed 'The Hengwrt Chaucer', some readers may be surprised to learn that 'the most precious manuscript in the Middle English language' – the oldest surviving copy of the *Canterbury Tales*, made about 1400 – is held at the National Library of Wales in Aberystwyth. Another Chaucer manuscript, *Boece,* his translation of Boethius's *Consolatio Philosophie*, of very similar date and 'quite extraordinary significance for English literature' also resides at Nat. Lib., as we familiarly refer to it. Both manuscripts came from the same source, identified by their catalogue entries. The *Tales* is MS Peniarth 392D, and *Boece* Peniarth 393D. The former, he says, is 'the most unmemorable reference to any world-class manuscript', though I cannot say Cotton Vitellius A15 springs readily to my mind. From about 1650 both had been part of the collection of the Vaughan family of Hengwrt, near Dolgellau, Gwynedd, which on the death of the last of the line passed to a distant relative, William Watkin Edward Wynne of Peniarth, Merionethshire. When Wynne's heir died in 1909, they were acquired by Sir John Williams (1840–1926), royal physician, who is described in the *Dictionary of Welsh Biography* as 'the principal founder of the National Library'. When Cardiff was increasingly becoming the magnet of things of cultural significance, Williams fought for the library to be established in Aber, and won. In 1909, he gave his manuscript collection to the new institution.

De Hamel's quest took him from Cambridge to Copenhagen, Munich to New York. Completing a Russian visa application for a visit to St Petersburg was a tedious business; otherwise the only reference to travel is the unconscionable length and duration of the train journey to Aberystwyth. There he finds that 'everyone can speak Welsh (and they do), impen-etrable to the English' so that 'it all feels as foreign as Finland'. 'Why do these English treasures languish in this distant hole?' seems to be implied. A less irritable response might perceive from the tone of his description that he found the seaside town and his reception at Nat. Lib. charming and amusing, as though at the station he had opened a portal into the past. Then again, I wonder whether, on reflection, he might think it rather shaming that Welsh is to him as foreign as Finnish. He is an uncommonly gifted man of formidable intellect, who doubtless has command of classical Latin and Greek, yet his education has not afforded him an opportunity to acquire one of the principal living languages of Britain – the British language, indeed. This is not his fault. It is the fault of Westminster governments of all times and kinds that take no pride in the survival of Welsh, and have done as little as possible (with a niggard hand and under duress) to support it.

As for the journey to Aberystwyth, I am reminded of the story of an old farmer from Gwynedd who is constantly nagged that for once in his life he really ought to see London. He finally yields to persuasion and takes a coach trip. On his return, stiff from the journey, family and friends ask what he thought of the great metropolis. 'London is quite interesting,' he says, 'but, you know, it's very remote.' The remoteness of London, with its vast accumulation of *national* treasures, from by far the greater part of the population of Britain is insufficiently considered and least of all by the so-called 'metropolitan elite'. It is a stunning irony that the British Library is more readily accessible from half of Europe than it is from much of Wales.

From the Journals of R. F. Langley

THE POET R. F. LANGLEY (1938–2011) was also, privately, a prolific prose writer. Extracts from his journals, which he began in 1969, first appeared in *PN Review* in 2002. The notes to Langley's *Complete Poems*, edited by Jeremy Noel-Tod, cite a number of unpublished journal entries that directly informed the writing of his verse.

1 APRIL 2006

Snowy mountains. White files of small clouds all parallel and stretching out over the Channel from the English coast, then inland over the fields, each cloud with its shadow lagging a little and a little to one side. Odd how they change shape so slowly as they move, holding out their thin texture in curls and fixed gestures, as if they were forgetting what they were doing and had been caught by a thought. Or you can steady yourself and see them in their meteorology – small pieces of cumulus boiled up over the land and carried by the wind, in their parallel streams, out to sea. Plate 2. Forms of Cumulus. The result of convection, heated ground from morning sunlight, thermals rise to, and through, their condensation level. Their duller fringes are the evaporating parts, held up as they disappear, slowly, whiter tops, very white and still sharp and confident for a while. Miniature events, risen, and now falling away, filing away, back to where we are coming from. England is warm. I read on the plane, my head falling forward again and again as I sleep. The neat little Fontana Modern Master on Freud by Wollheim, taken to fit into luggage and be worthwhile. I am still in early chapters – on the Theory of the Mind, phi, psi and omega neurons, systems of, interactions of, quantities determining pathways, all so impossible to believe even though the bright clouds outside the portholes behave and behave, in pathways, in quantities, moving to systems.

Glasgow SQE University

Entrance Examination

FRANK KUPPNER

FIRST PAPER
Normal terms and conditions apply.

1. So: this 'God' business. What's all that about?

2. Come on! There's something really too haphazard about all existence, isn't there?

3. What's that you've got on your head? Blood? Surely not *paint*?

4. How many of the people even in this very room are really as much in control as they are pretending to be?

5. But how on earth are we to meet even all these people?

6. Yes – we are all the results of the complicated workings of other people's private parts. But how often in our thus-derived lives do we ever truly *feel* that this undeniable fact is indeed the case?

7. And which of us has any specific or private right [rite?] *in the slightest* to be here?

8. These krillions of stars! (*Hum.*) Right. So. This one *here*, perhaps?

9. Don't you feel at all – like (you know?) – like the development of daily life itself is not, *ipso facto*, like some sort of *act of treachery* against the pure dead brilliant untimed planet as such? Eh? No? (What? Not even *metaphorically*?)

10. But to what extent are we aware even of the [implications of the [non-conscious?]] life we have actually been leading anyway?

11. Yes. Why does the whole thing so often seem so *otherwise*?

12. Where, for instance, does it all go to? [All of it! All of it!]

13. Do any of us really *want to remember* this bit?

14. Very well. Why didn't you just say that to begin with [– Lord]?

15. What could silence possibly be another name for? (Not the *word*. The actual *thing* [if any].)

16. I doubt whether Almighty God could exactly be said to have a distinct style – don't you?

17. Which reminds me: do you honestly think that all these celebrated 'great Greek and Roman writers' (so-called) were ever making terribly much of an effort *really*?

18. But then, which of us (for that matter) really believe that we are living two – or maybe even *three* – millennia in the past?

19. And how much of what they said so long ago did they [we?] ever really need?

20. It seemed infinitely more convincing when our own (never not adult) parents were doing it, did it not?

21. And which of us couldn't just as easily have died in one more routinely fluke childhood accident?

22. Yes. How many of them are in fact missing, Doctor?

23. Don't you too feel that I deserve so much better than this?

24. Of whom do you find it easiest to ask: is this the life that I *really want* to ruin?

25. Don't you agree, for instance, that (caring!) sexual relationships between staff and students are not always *necessarily* wrong?

26. Yes. Be *rigorously honest* here. Don't you find me at least a *little bit* attractive – particularly for someone of my own mature (though still fairly youthful!) age?

27. If there is only one real question, then what should that question be?

28. IS THIS [EVEN] PHYSICALLY POSSIBLE?

29. Could anyone else have done it if they had been you?

30. Eating plants and so forth! That's actually how it's [going to be] done, is it?

31. What? No such thing as a free lunch? They what exactly is the whole bloody Universe? (Yes! This must be it here!)

32. Could any real genius genuinely believe that 'the Universe which actually exists is probably only some sort of secondary effect of an impossible primary phenomenon'?

33. So – why should it not be the case that some force or other is taking something or other out on [us] personally?

34. After all, surely it profoundly nourishes the insecure, ravenous ego to have some of these *other people* more or less at its mercy, testifying tumultuously to its central importance for them? Doesn't everybody know that yet?

35. Or: estimate exactly how much of the trouble comes from those who aren't happy with who they are – and who ('since most of it is going on well below the surface, Tom' – *Di Veres*) can hardly even begin to work out quite why this is the case.

36. Can you nonetheless believe that opposing views are not necessarily negative?

37. Yes. So. Is one real world quite enough *in fact* [, Gabriela]?

38. Is the feeling that 'something is badly wrong here' never itself [badly? [sinfully? [Eh?]]] wrong?

39. Or perhaps you too feel, as 'a peculiarly sexy beasting' (Newoman) that thou art (look you!) something of an (essentially immaterial?) exception to the (merely physically real) Cosmos? No? Maybe not?

40. Might Life be 'a kind of pyrrhic victory over matter' (Pater)? Or even over non-existence itself? [*Itself*? What kind of self could that conceivably be? [And how, indeed, could it be any sort of *final* victory at all over anything whatsoever? (A?)]]

41. Hello? Hello? Is this me in here?

42. Dear me – a lot of your (m)utterances are really not so very hint-elegant, are they?

43. Can one possibly *decide* to be intelligent? Have you, for instance, by any [possibly fat?] chance, ever thought of making a [hopeless?] decision remotely like that yourself? [Do *please* tell us. We'd be absolutely *fascinated* to know.]

44. If you were God, would it matter terribly much to thee whether anything else really believed you were what you were or not? (Be *unusually* honest. [And coherent too, if that's actually possible.])

45. Just concentrate on getting this next bit right, eh?

46. But if you were a God who could bring into being out of nothing else [only?] a world in which sin and loss and suffering had to exist, would you nonetheless do it? Why?

47. Yes. One always has to *spoil* a Universe a little in order to start it, does one not? [And, if not, then how about: in order to *finish* it?]

48. Oh, indeed! And isn't it impressive just how substantial the completely imaginary can often (be made to [seem to]) be?

49. For, surely, in the last resort, nothing is not in principle within the limits of the Comprehensible?

[CORRECTION. (*Disregard the previous question, if necessary.*)

49. Surely, in the last resort, Nothing is not in principle within the limits of the Comprehensible?]

From the Archive

Issue 134, July–August 2000

MARKINGS

PATRICK MACKIE

From a contribution of three poems, including 'Extravagance' and 'Monogamy'. Fellow contributors to this issue include Anne Stevenson, Robert Minhinnick, R.F. Langley, Carola Luther, and Peter Scupham.

Everything is noticed. That is, everything happens twice.
It had been safer. Later on, amongst the paths,
after the images had ended, promises now seem
to have been made, or taken. The wind sweetened

transmission. Directions were given across the thickening
light, matters of left or right, narrow gates, choices in
darkness. The night's sky, a mass of hints, had an engrossing
coldness. Shh. I'm only talking about the weather.

Ways to Get About Busan

JOHN WILKINSON

for Rod Mengham

Day awaits the kindly figures: will our visitors accept
proposals as once they did? Provocative zeroes float.
    Roadsides hold the well-sorted
    denizens to their grid scales, well-satisfied,
    flashing tickets without limit of time.

On each surface section, the entertainment district
swept like a blush and faded, short order overtaken
    brought a playlist, new attachments,
    windswept, mindful, other side of the coin,
    one purely desert, the obverse aswarm.

For evidence a sallow crease plumes innovative cloud,
beach resorts, short squid, pails of slopping zeniths,
    sentiments that vaporise in perfume
    squalls, caprices of a passing shirt,
    no peg, no idol, focal point or polarity:

Could our visitors endure such abjection into virtue,
hand-held glare or touchscreen that foams with poly-
    valent zeroes, pop-ups and events
    shimmering in light tied to fluctuations
    in Shanghai, saffron, silk trousseau?

Stagger back towards a pleater in his clouds of steam,
the superintendent who'll collapse choking, much
    sought will go silent, tetherless
    rip dwelling cries out of heaps of stone,
    look: this is a ground plan for a kitchen –

drew a blind of lapses, dropouts twinkled on the pane,
losses pillowed what loss-bearers' loved foibles cast
    mocked under scrutiny, cherished bits
    injurious spurs grieve, a trilobite
    cricked neck hung weeping-on amidst

falbalas in their spun radish beds – the booster stage
nosed firmly on those left behind, force ready-ranked
    but yet unseated, shifting coloured
    beads, a regimen of spit and polish,
    aligning and then slotted brusquely

partygoing packs in housings between bracket breves,
the anchorless, those who sidestep species and genus.
    We catch it here first. Squeals as property
    gets clamped, plaintive hoots resound
    with geodetic data, red and gold flashes

pinned on for mating. Noise swirling in each amphora
between the ideograms of the actual, three or more,
    flushes stacks, retrieves such
    preferences which knowing best
    bring up a blackbird or a sandpiper,

visitors up to five like marked men were puzzling out
plugs of sediment, unreadable once overtones lift off
    ideograms devoid of sonic trace
    flash minatory above blank doors
    or calcified crash to a pavement:

boundary a white stone swooshes as a meteor imparts
viruses, splinters of the true cross, a murderous quiet
    evacuates the icon from its
    dark hollow eyes it hoists
    unblinking in heaven's nave.

Disks will dawn above the slamming bars, flawlessly
enamelled with a Pantone colour, semi-liquid states
    captured at high speed in varnish,
    processing in through-pass, print
    tokens, irises, electronic room keys,

rigid as medallions, wobbling into traffic signal order.
What will they leave below? Go back a step: emphasis
    calls out a flanged sidelong look,
    an eyebrow arches in a stroke thicket,
    through spurts of steam transmits

curving swallows to a lip that tremulous in coral pink
means a loudspeaker, no, an inarticulately adhesive
    heart-dithering trill, a living hand
    adjusts a lover's skew-whiff look,
    lifts his drink amidst the steam, you!

guerdoned at the last with shame, riddle out a range's
terrible ash when gates to be impaled on, bang closed,
    echo locked out of looped
    shunts, mountain passes shut, bends
    whose camber baffles kindly ones

flashed across an internal screen, will our visitors take
    Look: Flash/ Look: Flash/ Look:
    actual blanks, blanks that in action
sift like ash but name a tree upon a blank. It is an ash.
Would that it were an ash the palm still kept in hand.
    A cedar in an anatomical snuff-box.

Branches have been populated, gaps filled with birds,
while underneath Building 40, eighty storeys high,

arguments of art shrivel in their cages, staggered trees
braced in metal, hunch in mist and micro-particles.

The effortful remembrances tinkle as an unavailing
bird pipes at the empire, against their wall of concrete

pre-moulded sections, rows of windows not lit up
as dusk falls. The blushing sky would divorce the day.

The Golden Ratio

Poetry & Mathematics

EMILY GROSHOLZ

IN HIS BOOK *The Poetics of Space*, Gaston Bachelard talks about the house of childhood, the house we never leave because at first we live in it, and afterwards it lives on in us. The house of childhood organises our experience, first of all determining inside and outside, and then offering middle terms: the front porch and its steps are a middle term between the house and the town, while the back yard and garden are a middle term between the house and the wild. (In the proportion between two ratios expressed in A:B :: B:C (or 'A is to B as B is to C'), we call B the *middle term*, which brings A and C into clear relation.) It organises what is far away, because we measure 'away' by how far it is from home, how many hours or days of travel. Moreover, the windows of the house let in the distances, the dwindling train tracks, river or road, the fields and forest, even the cloudy-blue or starry heavens: they are set squarely on the walls within the window frames, as light comes through and we see what is outside. It also organises time. What lives in the basement or the attic? We ourselves do not eat or sleep or socialise or read there, though those rooms are part of the house: they are where we put the past, the discarded and the treasured. Finally, the house invites playing: the playroom with its gate and the fenced part of the backyard, enclosures where the toys are kept and children imitate the human activities of building and furnishing houses, admonishing and encouraging their dolls, rushing about on small basketball courts and soccer pitches, setting forth amidst the ceremonies of departure and return.

This brings me back to two songs. The first is, to my mind, the most beautiful of the poems in Robert Louis Stevenson's *A Child's Garden of Verses* (1885): 'Where Go the Boats?' As a child I owned a golden vinyl record with this poem on it, recorded as a song: thus I learned it by heart and I can still, and very often do, sing it. Many of the poems I know by heart I learned as songs, especially poems in other languages.

Dark brown is the river.
Golden is the sand.
It flows along forever,
With trees on either hand.

Green leaves a-floating,
Castles of the foam,
Boats of mine a-boating,
Where will all come home?

On goes the river
And out past the mill,
Away down the valley,
Away down the hill.

Away down the river,
A hundred miles or more,
Other little children
Shall bring my boats ashore.

The house where I grew up was not located by a river. However, earthbound as it was, my house was just a block south of the Main Line railroad tracks, in the suburbs of Philadelphia. We heard the train whistles, and the Doppler Effect lowering the pitch, all day long; it was my first, aural introduction to the sorrow of the Red Shift: why are all those galaxies leaving us? We were also a block north of the Lincoln Highway, one of the first transcontinental highways in the United States. Route 30, as it was designated under the auspices of the United States Numbered Highway system, established in 1926, ran all the way to San Francisco, and when my parents returned from California where my father had served in the Navy during the Korean War, that's the route they came home on. We had a painting of the cypresses 'the sailor wind / ties into deep sea knots' (as Robinson Jeffers wrote) at Point Lobos over our fireplace, and I retained a few fugitive memories of California and the long trip back home. So for me that road always led to California, as well as Exton (where the best ice cream place was), Downingtown (summer camp lay on its outskirts), and Lancaster (where the Amish people at the Farmers' Market came from), points west that seemed far, far away. On my first road trip in high school, I drove a friend past Lancaster, north to the Ephrata Cloister – which was like going to eighteenth-century southwest Germany, as I later discovered – and felt that I had achieved adulthood, navigating past the Pillars of Hercules into unknown waters. But I must return to early childhood.

As Tolkien wrote, in another of my beloved books *The Hobbit* (1937), 'The road goes ever, ever on.' So the Lincoln Highway set up a dialectic with my house, not least because Point Lobos was over the fireplace and my mother's most romantic, and often repeated, memories were of California and Hawaii: she was never able to travel much during most of her short life, except to the New Jersey beaches and to New England where she went to college and still had friends. Her stories were the other side of my father's silences, though he too had a trove of stories, set pieces with all the bitter absurdity of those in Joseph Heller's *Catch-22*. Drafted in World War II, and then again in the Korean War, my father spent seven years of his life crossing the great Pacific again and again in destroyers and tankers, seeking refuge from his terror and displacement in alcohol, at sea. And though he made it back home, like Odysseus, he was often there but not there, sitting in his armchair reading through tome after tome of Naval history and smoking the cigarettes that eventually bore him away again.

Geometry starts with the house and field and town centre, as we find it in Euclid, for Euclidean geometry is the study of *figures*. Here is a sampling of his definitions, from Book I of the *Elements*.

3 The extremities of a line are points. 4 A straight line is a

line which lies evenly with the points on itself. 5 A surface is that which has length and breadth only. 6 The extremities of a surface are lines. 13 A boundary is that which is an extremity of anything. 14 A figure is that which is contained by any boundary or boundaries.

The Thirteen Books of Euclid's Elements, tr. Thomas L. Heath (1956).

And then he gives us the circle, various triangles, the square, and the oblong, the rhombus, and various trapezia. This is the world of childhood: the yard is a rectangle; the house is a closed figure, a set of rectangles and triangles (the walls and roof) hemming in a cuboid; the lane is a bounded straight line; the center of town is a square. But the road is a line that goes on and on, like the river, like the train tracks that allow the train to glide so quickly, in a straight line at a constant speed, as the train whistle turns into a lament. The house is a finite figure, straight from the pages of Euclid, and thus a figure of finitude; but the road, or river, is not a figure, for 'it flows along forever'. Or rather, it is a figure after all, thanks to the linguistic red shift given to the term 'figure' by the ambiguities of English: it is a figure of the infinite.

And we see a foreshadowing of the expansion of geometry into the infinite in the seventeenth and nineteenth centuries in the last of Euclid's definitions, which he added to clarify the peculiar status of parallel lines.

23 Parallel straight lines are straight lines which, being in the same plane and being produced indefinitely in both directions, do not meet one another in either direction.

This definition doesn't limit itself to line segments; it involves co-planar lines that are 'produced indefinitely' and yet never meet. So we are invited to think about what happens to a line as it goes on and on: in the seventeenth century, Desargues, inspired by optics and a novel theory of perspective, was one of the founders of projective geometry, and proposed that all co-planar lines intersect: parallel lines just intersect at infinity, 'the point at infinity'. And Leibniz, following the work of Desargues and Pascal, took space itself as an object whose structure is revealed by studying the transformations of figures, and what remains invariant among the transformations: thus one could think of all the conic sections as variants of the circle. Indeed, in 1679, Leibniz briefly considered the possibility of spherical geometry (the easiest of the non-Euclidean geometries to understand, because navigation on earth more or less exemplifies it), based on the analogy between all lines in projective geometry intersecting (some in the point at infinity) and all geodesics on a spherical surface intersecting (a geodesic is the shortest distance between two points on a spherical surface and thus the analogue to a straight line in 'flat' Euclidean geometry). However, he veered off in another direction and left the explicit formulation of non-Euclidean geometry on a surface of constant positive curvature to the Hungarian mathematician Janos Bolyai in the nineteenth century, following upon the work of Euler and Gauss. Nikolai Lobachevsky worked out the non-Euclidean geometry on a surface of constant negative curvature around the same time, but entirely independently. And Bernhard Riemann,

building on the work of his teacher Gauss, came up with the generalised notion of a two dimensional surface (generalisable to *n*-dimensional surfaces) which launches geometry into the realm of topology.

If only everyone had decided to stop fighting in 1940, or 1945, or 1950 – my father could have kept on sailing east, around the south coast of India and then of Africa, and just come back along a geodesic to my mother and me. My mother used to sing me this lullaby, by Alfred Lord Tennyson.

Sweet and low, sweet and low,
Wind of the Western sea.
Blow, blow, breathe and blow,
Wind of the Western sea.
Over the rolling waters go,
Come from the dying moon, and blow,
    Blow him again to me;
While my little one, while my pretty one, sleeps.

[...] Father will come to his babe in the nest,
Silver sails all out of the west
    Under the silver moon:
Sleep, my little one, sleep, my pretty one, sleep.

Like a baby on its mother's breast, one can always dream. The house governs the poetics of space (inflected by time – and eventually Riemann's geometry provides a model for Einstein's space-time); the road and river govern a poetics of time (inflected by space – for we must all go home again, whether we can or can't, in fact or in imagination, sooner or later). And what child does not thrill to the romance of departure, which is after all what eventually he or she prepares to do: depart from the house of childhood, aided and abetted by romance.

During my twenties, I was lucky enough to travel often to Europe, where I studied the art and architecture that links Minoan Civilisation (c. 3500–1500 BCE) to classical Greece and Rome, thence to medieval Europe and the Renaissance (c. 1500 CE). Here is the great irony: to escape the square of the house of my childhood, I launched myself on rivers of air from Philadelphia to London, on traintracks from London to Paris to Rome to Brindisi, on Mediterranean currents from Brindisi to Patras and from Athens to Heraklion, and soared above five millennia. What did I find? Again and again, at the heart of the matter, I re-discovered the square! And all the reasons why we can, and must, go home again.

The square is often nestled in the golden ratio (symbolised by the Greek letter *phi*, φ). Two magnitudes stand in the golden ratio if their ratio is the same as the ratio of their sum to the larger of the magnitudes. So, assuming A > B > 0, we can write the proportion of the two ratios this way:

$$A : B :: A + B : A$$
(or 'A is to B as A plus B is to A')

Note that A is the middle term between B and A+B in this case. We can also define φ (which is, like √2, a quadratic irrational number) by using the late medieval trick of reconceptualising ratios as fractions and proportions as equations:

$$\varphi = A / B = (A+B)/A = (1 + \sqrt{5}) / 2$$

And finally, we retrieve the square tucked into a golden rectangle, which illustrates the golden ratio: the yellow side of the square is A, the purple top of the adjacent rectangle is B, so the longer side of the golden rectangle is A+B, and its shorter side is A. In this particular diagram, one stipulates that A=1, so that you can see especially clearly why $\varphi = (1 + \sqrt{5}) / 2 = 1.6180339887...$

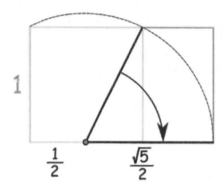

Two places where I arrived on my travels made an especially deep impression on me, so that I feel as if I could relive the very moment when I first beheld them. One was the Parthenon, on its hilltop overlooking Athens, where in the summer of 1970 I followed the shade of Socrates around, listening to him use *reductio ad absurdum* (that paradoxically valid deductive argument form) to make the citizens of his city puzzled, reflective and ultimately philosophical. Recall that his student Plato was convinced that mathematics was the middle term between Becoming and Being.

I kept a journal, and later I turned those journal entries into a narrative poem, *Cypress and Bitter Laurel*, which was eventually published in *The Reaper* (Vol. 17) by Mark Jarman and Robert McDowell. Here is that moment, recorded in the iambic pentameter I employed almost unconsciously:

Such an odd life we lead, the life of tourists
(And of spies, anthropologists and poets),
Moving slowly through the world's locations,
Transparent, unremarkable, all eyes.
[...]
Yesterday, we got up at five, to see
The Acropolis in the very earliest light.
Large enough to count as monumental,
Small enough to be visible all at once,

The Parthenon stood white against the sky
And taught us both a lesson in proportion
Even in ruins, its roof blasted away.
For what remains is so insistently formal,
The series of marble steps and columns require
Completeness in the act of the mind's eye.

The second place was Notre Dame in Paris: there it was again, the golden rectangle, and another embodiment in stone of the golden ratio and its iterations.

Three years later, in 1973, I bicycled around Normandy with Henry Adams's *Mont-Saint-Michel and Chartres* (1904) in my backpack, and then around Burgundy, with various writings by Viollet-le-Duc and the memoirs of my beloved Colette. A few months after that, starting graduate school at Yale University, I discovered Otto von Simson's *The Gothic Cathedral* (1956) under the tutelage of Karsten Harries. Adams and Simson both refer to the *Sketchbook* of Villard de Honnecourt, a thirteenth-century mason and architect from Picardy. On one page, he includes the following geometrical diagrams; the second (in red) shows how to halve the square (or, going in the opposite direction, how to double the square), as he analyses the ground plan of a cloister.

This diagram is especially significant because it recalls the construction in Plato's *Meno* where Socrates leads an unlettered, unschooled slave boy to this very construction just by asking him questions, and then suggests that any human soul has access to mathematics: it is the middle term that orients us toward the eternal. (This of course means that everybody should be able to go to university, women are good at mathematics, and nobody should be a slave.)

Von Simson asserts, 'the Gothic builders [...] are unanimous in paying tribute to *geometry* as the basis of their art. This is revealed even by a glance at Gothic architectural drawings [...] they appear like beautiful patterns of lines ordered according to geometrical principles. The architectural members are represented without any indication of volume, and, until the end of the fourteenth century, there is no indication of space or perspective. The exclusive emphasis on surface and line confirms our impressions of actual Gothic buildings [...] With but a single basic dimension given, the Gothic architect developed all other magnitudes of his ground plan and elevation by strictly geometrical means, using as modules

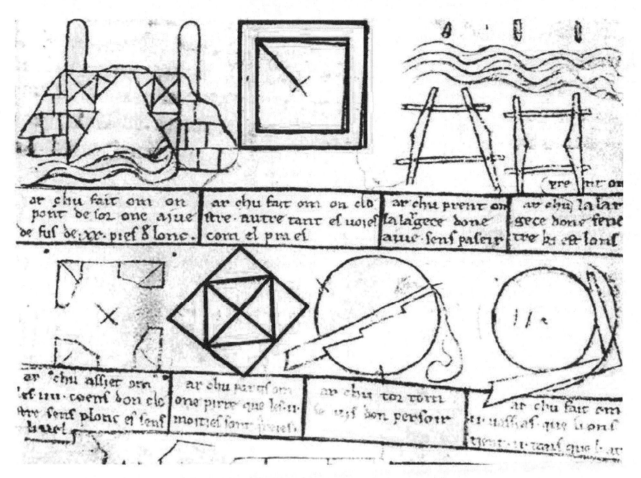

certain regular polygons, above all the square.' And a bit later he adds, 'The church is, mystically and liturgically, an image of heaven.' One expression of that order is mathematical structure, manifest in both architecture and music. St Augustine, c. 400 CE, invoked the science and art of music, because it was based on mathematics. (Pythagoras influenced Plato, and St Augustine was in turn influenced by Neoplatonism, despite his conversion to Christianity.) The most admirable ratio, he claimed, was $1:1$, equality, symmetry, and unison; next in rank were the ratios $1:2$ (the octave), $2:3$ (the fifth) and finally $3:4$ (the fourth). Just as the stone squares in their golden rectangles are beautiful and stable, so the notes in their admirable ratios are consonant. Augustine, von Simson tells us in *The Gothic Cathedral*, loved both architecture and music 'since he experienced the same transcendental elements in both'.

Later, he tells us that Villard's book contains 'not only the geometrical canons of Gothic architecture, but also the Augustinian aesthetics of 'musical' proportions. In one of his drawings, the ground plan of a Cistercian church, 'the square bay of the side aisles is the basic unit or module from which all proportions of the plan are derived [...] Thus the length of the church is related to the transept in the ratio of the fifth $(2:3)$. The octave ratio $(1:2)$ determines the relations between side aisle and nave, length and width of the transept, and [...] of the interior elevation as well. The $3:4$ ratio of the choir evokes the musical fourth; the $4:5$ ratio of nave and side aisles taken as a unit corresponds to the third; while the crossing, liturgically and aesthetically the

center of the church, is based on the $1:1$ ratio of unison, most perfect of consonances.' Von Simson goes on to explain in some detail how the architect of Notre Dame de Chartres elaborated on this structure in surprisingly innovative ways ('he turned to advantage the restrictions that tradition imposed upon his design') that allowed the vault of Chartres to be sprung at a much greater height than that of any of its predecessors. It was the first cathedral where the flying buttresses were aesthetically as well as structurally part of the overall design. Moreover, the golden ratio occurs in the figures of the west façade, as well as in the elevation: 'The height of the piers [...] is 8.61 m. The height of the shafts above (excluding their capitals) is 13.85 m. The distance between the base of the shafts and the lower string-course is 5.35 m. The three ratios $5.33 : 8.61 : 13.85$ are very close approximations indeed to the ratios of the golden section.' The dimensions of the elevation are also closely related to those of the ground plan. And so von Simson sums up: 'Medieval metaphysics conceived beauty as the *splendor veritas*, as the radiant manifestation of objectively valid laws.'

This is the poem I wrote, inspired by the churches of Normandy, in particular one especially lovely set of ruins in Jumièges:

[...] An ancient abbey stands in Jumièges.
The western towers, twin battlements
Against the tides of darkness, still remain,
But every wall is gutted, overgrown,
And the high roof, the paradigm of heaven,
Is long since stormed away.

Between the nave and choir there is no stair,
No screen to keep the crowds from their desire.
Only a copper beech, the prince of trees,
Whose monumental bole could bear
The manifold thin nervures of the air,
Divides the floor. The leaves divide the sky
In panes of bronze which fan
Around a spectral cross of red and green,
So the lost vault becomes a sheer
Translucent window, and the blue between
The blue of distance, as it ought to be [...]

Sometimes I think that the closest I have come to heaven were moments when I found myself standing in the nave of Chartres, looking up; but that was not just because of the radiant geometry and arithmetic manifest in the cathedral's stones. The cathedral is also astonishingly luminous: the great architect of Chartres also replaced solid walls, to an unprecedented extent, with the transparent walls of stained-glass windows. The clerestory is the upper part of the nave and choir and transepts: because it rises above the lower roofs its windows admit a flood of light, which animate the colours of the stained glass (as James tells us in his rhapsodic Chapter VIII of *Mont-Saint-Michel and Chartres*, 'The Twelfth-Century Glass'). And James reminds us that Villard sketched the western Rose Window at Chartres. When we look through the windows of the house of childhood, we see the town we live in and the woods and fields beyond, and the sky above, which sometimes (especially when it fills with wheeling stars) becomes a figure for heaven. But when we look 'through' the windows of Chartres, we see heaven: there it is. Thus as I look back on other poems I've written that include cathedrals, I notice that images of their windows evoke not only the sky, but also the edge of a forest backlit by the rising or setting sun as it scores the horizon with its slanting, golden light. The Clerestory: a middle term between earth and heaven.

Three poems

LAURA SCOTT

---

and Pierre?

With his ripe face like one of those pale freckled pears
you hold in your hand and his mind shuddering across it

like a bruise – he's legible to all the world. With his great legs,
broad and strong as the trees, he walks in and out of chapters

smelling of eau de cologne, or an animal that sleeps in a barn.
With his long fingers running across the stubble on his jaw,

he listens to the black Russian rain before he picks up his pen.
With his eyes so blue you'd think he'd drunk the sky down

with all that champagne, he watches the soldiers (red epaulettes
and high boots) drag that boy to the place where they shoot him.

He watches the boy pull his loose coat tight before he sags and slides
down the post. And when it's all over, he watches them roll him

gently into the hole with the others and before he can look away,
he sees, there in the earth, the boy's shoulder still moving.

Can't stand them

loathe them, always have, ever since
I was a child. Probably something to do with the wretched

nightingale in that story they used to read to me, piercing
its heart on a thorn and singing the white rose red before

it dies and its little corpse falls to the ground. The fleshy ones
are the worst, sucking up all the rain and all that cellulose,

or whatever its called, swelling inside them and the way
I can't stop myself cutting into them with my nail to leave

a crescent-shaped mark on their stems. And then the smell
they leave in the water in the bottom of the vase, the way

it curls into my nostrils. Lilies are so obvious, so banal,
but the hydrangeas with their heads as big as cabbages,

obsequiously bowing to me, like supplicants every time
I walk past. I like it when the rain bruises their tiny petals.

To the Trees

quick and slick
        and full of you,
the you I don't want,
                the you that brims over, brims under my lines, the you I can't
remake, reshape,
        the you I —
    just leave it, drop it, walk away. There's nothing to see here.

Go to the trees,
        I always go to the trees, but let's go
to the tree outside my window,
        the one standing on its own, away from all the others,
the one with the great arms stretching up

the one with too many fingers spreading themselves
        into shapes so the fierce birds might come to them. Too many for what?

To be just pointing at the sky,
        to be just making shapes for the birds?

They must be a trace of something,
        of some hand, some principle urging them on –

maybe Maths or God
        and God knows we don't want to go down that road
            do we?

    Just look at the trees.

I wish I didn't know any rules, any at all, and then my poems,
        or this poem at least,
would move, would soar, would hover and break
        into thousands and thousands
                of pieces of white material.

Three Poems

ANJALI YARDI

If Only

if only the children
of Iraq
Afghanistan
Syria

were whales
or elephants
tigers
or gazelles

if only
childlife
were a fashionable cause

if only countries
came with labels:
No children have been harmed
to preserve this polity.

Oymyakon

Oymyakon on the Indigirka river,
coldest town on earth where geography upends
the laws of physics and hills above
are warmer than the sunken valley.
You'd think no one would choose
to live here, but natives love it.

When the air bristles with ice crystals
they call the rustle of freezing vapour
the whisper of stars. Minus thirty is
balmy weather – the sky rings
with the laughter of children and the thwack
of axes chopping firewood and ice-blocks.

Houses stand on stilts over shifting permafrost.
A hole under the floorboards does for a fridge.
Shaggy horses fat as sheep stomp and snuffle
in frozen paddocks. Food is horse flesh and river fish
fresh, frozen, smoked or salted. Mare's milk fermented
makes mild, frothy kumis the local drink.

When nature fast-forwards in the nightless short
summer, you can watch grass grow up to three inches
a day like a sped-up film. Decay is slow.
Leaves frozen in the Pleistocene are still
decomposing. Sky burials were common
once with corpses left in trees like rotting fruit

but progress brought cemeteries. To gouge a grave
out of rock-hard permafrost, it must be slowly
melted down and dug, bonfire and shovel
used by turns for days. Even so, a sudden thaw
can bring long buried bodies bobbing to the surface
in their coffin boats, looking fresh-faced as the newly dead.

Siberian Burial Mound

In her twenties when they sealed her tomb
with a heap of boulders in the long summer grass
on the Ukok Plateau, she lay undisturbed
for twenty-four centuries, preserved
by the strangest miracle. The slow sluice

of rainwater seeping between cairn stones
filled and froze the underground chamber
into a glassy time-capsule. The ice kept
everything: silk, wool, felt, leather, wood, skin,
their colours, even the smell of wet wool and damp leather.

Six sacrificed horses leant against the walls,
their coats still glossy. Goat meat in a yak-horn dish
on a wooden table. In a coffin hollowed
from a single log lay her body in the posture of sleep,
exquisitely dressed in silk and gold jewellery.

Her face and neck were bare bone
but embalming had succeeded with the rest.
Tall for her time, she had long tapering fingers.
Blue tattoos pricked out in soot, brightened
on her pale parchment skin, covering arm

and shoulder in fabulous swirls of imagery,
beasts real and mythical to empower and protect.
Who she was remains a mystery. A woman
buried alone with full funeral honours argues high status.
Not a warrior for no weapons lay beside her.

A Pazyryk princess perhaps. Or priest. Or poet.
For they are thought to have honoured poets,
keepers of memory, fashioners and retailers
of epic sagas that, like the congealing ice,
held fast through time their fragile stories.

Do You Hear What I'm Saying?

Overheard in New Haven

SUJATA BHATT

I literally know my friends will be there.
We are blessed.
We are not.
Well compared to –

She's not a particularly nice person
but she hasn't done anything bad to you.
Even I don't really like her.

It's called Human Studies.
Okay, now you can say it.

I don't need to talk to my mom about anything.
I can hear it all in my head.

I just don't feel comfortable.
It just got worse. It's so bad.
It's frustrating, irritating –
What's happening?

My mom too. It's insane.
It's funny the way she talks about things
and the way her eyebrows go.

Oh my God! If you need a doctor
just let me know.
You look really nice though.
She would have been upset.
She looked terrible.

You need good character.
She complicated it.

It takes thirty-five minutes
or maybe fifteen minutes.
I think you should write this for your essay.
You know my mother says
such and such.

So please let me in.
You know you're having a bad day.
My mom is so obsessed about it.

You know my dad never
does anything in the kitchen
but he's so organised.
We have all this bottled up *angst*.
I can't imagine.
Oh yeah, yeah, live in the moment.
So I said, 'okay dad' –

Oh my God! But there's an art to learning.
Okay, I don't do that.

It's not like they're an aristocratic family.
It's my grandmother.
I didn't know this.

And one day I went out in shorts,
you know athletic shorts
and I wore flip flops and a hat
and sunglasses. But still –
Yeah, I know, I was super nicely dressed
but I wore flip flops you know for comfort.
There are parties where you go in jeans.
She's the most stylish person I have seen.

They dress to go to the mall,
you know just to buy bread.
And you run into everyone you know.
I mean I always wear a hat.

I don't live there. I don't even go back.
We need to go where people don't dress well.

Do you hear what I'm saying?

They have all these rules,
all these tricks.

I can't eat when I want to.
I can't drink when I want to.

The last two weeks I was going out
every night, drinking four to five beers
or very high caloric drinks.
But I can lose weight very easily
if I go on a diet.
I used to be a lot thinner
so I have all these nice clothes that are too tight now.
My shoulders are out of proportion.
It's so annoying.
My mom wasn't interested.
But if you wear a hat
it'll totally change your look.

What's Found in Translation

KAREN VAN DYCK

AFTER READING AND WRITING about Greek poetry for over thirty years I was impressed by the quality and intensity of artistic output in response to the recent social and economic crisis. It was unlike anything I had seen since the poetry that came out of the Dictatorship (1967–1974). As in that period, the strong presence of women poets was palpable. There were poems I felt needed to be translated, poems that had something to say to a larger audience outside Greece. More than anything, *Austerity Measures: The New Greek Poetry* is an anthology of poems as translations.

The term 'Austerity Measures', although it has come to be used as an economic term for cutbacks, refers more generally to the sense of having less to go around, as well as to losing something – a standard of living, an idea of Europe, a glorious past. 'Measures', though, has another meaning in poetry and music, especially in Greek where the word μέτρα (*metra*) also means metre. In this capacity it suggests that restrictions can be strategically reinvented. Austerity can be the measure of the possible. The practice of translation underscores the double edge of such productive disability. While a translation never gives us back the source text intact, it can create its own kind of abundance elsewhere in another language and culture. Though I first imagined 'Austerity Measures' as a title in English, its appropriateness was clinched when the editor of the Greek edition Stavros Petsopoulos also saw its potential. 'Μέτρα λιτότητας' (*Metra litotitas*) was a term embedded in the political discourse of the times, yet deeply poetic. It could help challenge the strict divide between belles-lettrism and social realism. At so many different levels, then, the anthology is about translation.

Reading through hundreds of collections and online blogs I was struck by how many poems written in the past decade in Greek refer to the rather obscure lotus eaters who sidetrack Odysseus with their drugged-out diet. Repeatedly the lotus eaters appear as a way of commenting on a certain aimlessness and ennui, but also of imagining an alternative future by forgetting both the present and recent past. In Chloe Koutsoumbeli's poem 'Penelope III', ancient myths clearly aren't working anymore:

It is not the Laestrygonians, nor the lotuses
which keep him far from her
[...]
It is that in the ancient world
by now it gets dark early
the earth isn't flat
and men sometimes get lost

(tr. A. E. Stallings, p. 314. All translations are from *Austerity Measures* unless otherwise noted.)

Kyoko Kishida is even more suspicious about the impasse Greece has reached:

Why do we still use the adverb 'stoically'?

Respect?
For whom?
The lotus eaters?

(tr. Rachel Hadas, p. 151)

Her collaborator Jazra Khaleed responds as if in an email, 'Re: Lotus Eaters', pushing her to see the opportunity offered by this situation:

Do not grieve for those who remain
Grieve for those who depart
Save your pity for Odysseus
Unite with the lotus eaters.

(tr. Peter Constantine, p. 173)

After all, it is the lotus eaters who enjoy peaceful coexistence, more promising than Odysseus, the wily warrior who leaves his companions in the lurch. The poet Phoebe Giannisi takes this view even further in her poem, 'Lotus Eaters II':

the medicine a flower
the medicine is the medicine
forgetfulness is every moment a brand new beginning
it's I don't know where I come from I don't want to return
the medicine is always now always now.

(tr. Angelos Sakkis, p. 119)

What matters for these poets is what happens when you forget, what happens when what you had is lost. Translation also involves forgetting in order to create something new. It is less about what is lost than what is found. The feminism of Koutsoumbeli's Penelope poem, for example, is more pronounced in Stallings's translation than in the original Greek. Where Koutsoumbeli simply has people (*anthropoi*), Stallings writes, '*men* sometimes get lost'. The conditions of austerity create room for alternative interpretations of poems through translation.

*

Compiling the anthology turned out to be a bigger project than I could have anticipated – over fifty poets, most under the age of fifty, and half as many translators. What emerged wasn't simply a list of the already anointed and awarded, but a whole terrain of poetry being written in Greek in the past decade – in Athens, on islands, in small towns, along the borders, and outside Greece. Poetry was happening everywhere, not just in the usual places. Poets in one arena had no idea about the work of poets in another. The organisation of the anthology showcases this distribution. Rather than chronological, alphabetical, or thematic, it highlights venues of poetic activity – where poetry is happening – from magazines to small presses to online blogs. The different spaces of production are arranged to show off, not only what is happening in Greece, but also what can happen through translation when this poetry hits the streets of London or New York. I chose poems and translations, not poets or translators. The project was about mapping poetry scenes, a what's where, rather than a who's who.

Anthologies are all about the art of ordering, bringing out an argument by grouping certain poets together, juxtaposing poems that continue a line of thought, and although in what follows I move section by section, choosing a poem from each and making a few comments about why it is exemplary of broader trends, for the most part I am concerned with what the poem as a translation makes possible. I focus on what I consider the most salient feature of this new poetry – its multiethnic, multilingual cosmopolitanism and then go for examples that showcase how something we usually think is destined to be lost in translation can actually be a way of connecting up disparate traditions – formal issues such as line length or the shape of a poem or issues of literary tradition and convention like intertextual references, proper names, linguistic register and codeswitching. I thought about putting first the less-known online poets like Khaleed and Kishida so as to shock readers out of any expectation of Greek clichés like marble columns, sea, and sun, but my editor at Penguin, Donald Futers, relayed an interesting observation. Most readers, he said, thumbing through books of poetry in bookstores, open to the middle. This is where you can catch them by surprise. So I kept with my plan to move from Athens and established literary magazines to the more offbeat literary collectives to online poetry, to poetry in the provinces and on the borders, to outside Greece altogether.

I began with poets working within the Greek poetry tradition and saved the Antifa, in-your-face poetry for later, although even in the first section I chose work that comes at the tradition at a slant. A poem from Yiannis Efthymiades's series about a man falling from the World Trade Center – twenty-seven poems of twenty-seven lines (three stanzas of nine lines) of twenty-seven syllables – is indicative. Traditional in its attention to metre and its references to the poetry of the nineteenth-century national poet Dionysis Solomos, as well as Nobel Laureate George Seferis, the poem is also wildly untraditional in its subject matter and the length of its line. It demonstrates a key theme of this new poetry: the interlacing of local and global. Greek poetry doesn't have to be about Greece. The poem captures the fear and unknown of the times, but it is not at all clear where the crisis is located – Greece? America? Everywhere? No tragedy, it appears, is national any longer.

all of you think I was scared shitless that's why I dove head
    first into the abyss
god what idiots for once I took my life into my own hands
    and let myself
drop provocative like in front of their eyes immense ghoul-
    ish I stick my tongue out
then in that last moment I see a girl with a sad look in the
    midst of the crowd
nothing special to remember about her just that she was a
    sad girl that's all
two summers ago or two years after we could've fallen in
    love yeah could've

though this chance in a lifetime didn't come to fruition how
    many ever do
and so in the end I won't be here but the girl sure will what
    simple logic yours
the kind of logic I repeated proudly ad nauseam for so many
    years

(tr. Karen Van Dyck, p. 21)

My translation is an attempt to register this postnational moment in the language of a country caught in a new post-9/11 patriotism. I decided to follow Efthymiades with his attention to counting and measuring. He could get away with a big number like twenty-seven since Greek is an inflected language where long lines can still sound conversational and effortless, but English needed a shorter line. I chose twenty so I could break the line into nine- and eleven-syllable sections and inscribe the fatal date of the terrorist attack. This shorter line with its caesura also allowed me to create a style that could be reinserted back into English establishing a relation, not so much between local and global at the level of literary tradition, but between 'us' and 'them' at the level of register: street vernacular versus specialised jargon; 'scared shitless' versus 'didn't come to fruition'. Whereas Efthymiades's lengthening of the traditional fifteen-syllable line was a way of worlding Greek poetry and making room for non-Greek references and themes, my shorter, but equally fixed line would make the contrast more about class and enable me to jumble the discourses of bureaucrats and your regular Joe.

As well as syllable count, line length and the visual shape of the poem are important factors that contribute to how this poetry rewrites Greek literature. It wasn't necessary to reproduce form, but attention to form could be a catalyst for introducing new interpretations in the translation. The next section introduces a more offbeat scene, still Athens-based, a group that believes in poetry as a kind of alchemy turning poison into medicine, as the double sense of the Greek word φάρμακον (farmakon) confirms. These poets draw on the literary tradition but tend to focus on the work of poets from the Dictatorship generation like Katerina Anghelaki Rooke and Jenny Mastoraki. Phoebe Giannisi reinvents Anghelaki-Rooke's classic poem about Penelope, especially these lines:

and I will cut
with words
the threads that bind me
to the particular man
I long for
until Odysseus becomes the symbol of Nostalgia
sailing the seas of every mind.

(tr. Karen Van Dyck, in Anghelaki-Rooke 2009, p. 8)

Giannisi responds by turning elegy into activity. Her Penelope is athletic, breathless:

She is passionate about swimming every day in the pool
up and down the same lane over and over the pool keeps
her alive swimming in the pool sustains her the continual
back and forth the rhythmic breathing the hands and feet
synchronised with the head going in and out of the water the
head repeatedly going up and down for air breathing in and

out resting sometimes in the lane the tiles under the surface in the light the foreign bodies monsters with their caps and flippers the chlorine water the sky over the cypresses the pool keeps her alive the continual song the counting one two three four five six seven eight nine fifteen nineteen kicks to a lap and turn the song of counting the repetition turns the pool song to stone saves me saves me from the knowledge he doesn't love me

(tr. Karen Van Dyck, p. 115)

While Giannisi's poem is written in free verse much like Anghelaki-Rooke's, I turned the translation into a concrete poem in the shape of a swimming pool to make it even more breathless: without lines the reader is obliged to find her own place to breath. Translations often up the ante to make their point.

While the *Farmakon* group knows its predecessors, the poets associated with *Teflon* magazine like Khaleed and Kishida wipe the slate clean, taking on Arabic and Japanese pseudonyms and translating poetry from all over the world – from Amiri Baraka to Keston Sutherlund to Etel Adnan. During a reading at Columbia University last spring, Khaleed responded to a question about his influences by denouncing any connection to the Greek poetry tradition. His poem 'Why Greek Poetry Bores Me' insists on using lowercase initials to refer to leading post-World War II poets: 'the anagnostakes, the patrikious and the / varnales, all of whom want / to weigh me down / with their failure' (2016, 49).

Proper names create an interesting set of problems when it comes to what's lost and found in translation. While the poets' names in Khaleed's poem would need a note in order to be legible in English, the name of a prominent journalist, 'pretenderis', again with a lowercase initial, was too easy to search on Google and therefore too much of a libel risk, according to Penguin (170-1). Max Ritvo, the translator, agreed to remove the name, although he kept the play on the word 'pretend': 'The pretenders! Angels of TV! Tarry, pretender, with smiles unscary!' By far the freest translation in the anthology, really an adaptation, Ritvo shows that what is and isn't legible in translation can nonetheless be an excuse for experimentation.

Another section focuses on a new narrative strain in Greek poetry. A poem called 'Nightmare Pink' by Elena Penga could just as well be flash fiction, a short story or a monologue in a play:

It's raining. Here. There. Where you're singing. Raining very hard. I'm sitting in the house in a deep swivel chair. It's nighttime. I spin the chair around and listen to the rain. You're singing. The rain is loud enough to hear. I listen. To the rain. Another person arrives. With a pink lampshade. Brand new. He switches off the light, unscrews the bulb, takes off the black shade, puts on the pink one, then switches the light back on. We sit bathed in pink light and talk about shades. Lampshades. I open the balcony doors. You're singing. But the rain is louder. It comes into the house. Hits the lampshades. Knocks over the lights. Collides with reality. The cherry trees in the neighbor's yard haven't had fruit for years. Four men enter carrying sticks. They enter the neighbor's yard along with the rain. They've come to discipline the trees and chop them down if they don't blossom. I watch the men hit the trees. I watch the rain hit the men.

(tr. Karen Van Dyck, p. 247)

Important here is the way the everyday has everything to say about larger issues of power and control. Translation can make a difference by simply including prose in an anthology of poems and calling it a poem.

Intertextuality is another testing ground for translators. Whereas in the poems by Efthymiades and Giannisi the question of literary references was reworked at the levels of register and typography, it is also possible to translate intertextuality by creating references to literature in the new culture, replacing one intertext with another. Glykeria Basdeki's poem rewrites a well-known Balkan folk song about a stonemason who builds his wife into a bridge as a sacrifice:

LET DOWN THE CHAIN

To drag up
the bones

The ropes
spit
milk

Don't even think
about it darling

No miracles
for you
here

Even if you're
the master builder's
wife

No one's got
pull
in Bondageville

(tr. Karen Van Dyck, p. 281)

Like Penga's disciplining of the cherry trees, this poem talks about the crisis without actually referring to it. A social structure or conjuncture can be perceptible in poetry indirectly, through the transformation poets make of prior cultural materials. Here it is the sense of being trapped created by the reference to the macabre folksong and the feminist revision it enables. Because few Anglophone readers will know this ballad or its refrain to 'pull up the chain', my translation draws on another tale of female incarceration, 'Rapunzel, Rapunzel, let down your hair', while also giving 'pull' the metaphorical sense of corrupt leverage.

The final section brings together poets who live between cultures and languages – whether Greeks who live in Paris, Bergen or Nicosia or others who have made their home in Athens but come from Bulgaria, Iran, or Serbia. Often these in-between writers continue to have lives as writers elsewhere. Elena Penga and Iana Boukova both have short stories in the most recent volume of Dalkey Archive's *Best European Fiction*, but while Penga is described as hailing 'from Greece', Boukova is 'from Bulgaria' (Davis, 2017). If my anthology were to continue with its concentric circles reaching further and further away from Athens, it would then move outside to diasporan writers who write Greek poetry in other languages. In this sense Theodoris Chiotis's anthology *Futures: Poetry of the Greek Crisis* is a companion volume in that it mixes his own translations from the Greek with poems written originally in English by diasporan and expat poets (2015). I decided, however, to keep *Austerity Measures* focused on poetry written in Greek, even if with a fair share of Gringlish, Gralbanian and Grurkish: foreign words are scattered throughout the anthology. Stathis Baroutsos's poem 'Txt message' is actually written in the Roman alphabet (182), and Peter Constantine's translation highlights this choice with his SMS-ese: 'Big night 2nite' (183). But it is the sound and rhythm of Greek in Mehmet Yashin's Turkish, made visible in Barış Pirhasan's translation through the intermixing of German and English (406–7), that cements the multilingual game-change this generation embraces.

The collection is an attempt to explore how translations register the distinctive features of the contemporary Greek poetry scene. The bilingual format emphasises this point. Translation as a hermeneutic practice is laid bare when the Greek poem and the English version are set alongside each other, although what may register on mono-alphabetic readers is the estrangement of how delirious Greek letters look. Still, many choices are evident to readers without Greek as they look from left to right and back again. The translations clearly have their own form and style in English. They often don't line up with the Greek: one text is longer than another, shaped differently. Because formal constraints and literary critical concerns, even when tied to a particular poetic tradition, can suggest new modes of expression in the receiving language, translation requires not only a deep understanding of different forms, practices, and traditions, but also an openness to how literatures and cultures are always crisscrossing and sharing with each other. As with any creative endeavor, translation requires a willingness to play, to push things more in one direction or another, to pull back, accelerate, decelerate. Contrary to common opinion, the practice of translation is rarely about equality.

What's found in translation? At the most basic level, everything. As Phoebe Giannisi puts it, 'it's I don't know where I come from I don't want to return', or as Jazra Khaleed implores, 'Unite with the lotus eaters.' Anglophone readers, more specifically, will discover a different understanding of Greek poetry, no longer Cavafy, Seferis, Elytes, and Ritsos. And, with this shift away from the Generation of the Thirties, the notion of literature as a national institution is unsettled. The poems and translations I have gathered are not linked to one nation or another; they don't insist on Ancient Greek roots or divide themselves over whether they are Greek, Balkan, European, American. Rather they are both / and / plus Arabic, African. They overspill the containers of what is and isn't Greek, is and isn't poetry. An important internationalism was achieved through modernism and the likes of Nobel Laureates such as Seferis and Elytes, but it was in the name of literature as a national project and solely within a Eurocentric frame. It was powerful enough so that no poetry since, even that of Anagnostakis, Sachtouris,

Anghelaki-Rooke and Mastoraki, all with translations published by reputable presses in English, made much of a difference in the ensuing decades. The new generation that appears in *Austerity Measures*, however, seems to be changing the dominant anglophone reception of Greek poetry, joining forces through translation with poets around the world and showing that the Greek crisis is global. Their translingual, transnational view reverberates in Greece so that Greek poetry is not the same for Greek readers either.

*

Only after the anthology was finished did it become clear to me how the drama of borders, migrants, and a sea impossible to patrol, now so much in the news, had emerged in Greek poetry some time ago. Literature often tells us what will happen before it happens. Poetry, more than other genres, plays the role of a Cassandra. What is striking is *how* the soothsaying in this poetry involved upending the older model of disinterested modernism. It insisted on talking about the troubles, however indirectly. It wasn't possible to let boatfuls of migrants drown and to build barbed wire fences and detention centres without serious repercussions for everyone. Given the recent resurgence of separatisms –Grexit, Brexit, Trump's wall on the Mexican border – the message is only more urgent now. We need poetry, and poetry in translation, to tell us things we can't know otherwise, and if we don't pay attention, it is at our own peril. As William Carlos Williams says in the epigraph to the anthology, 'It is difficult to get the news from poems / yet men die miserably every day / for lack / of what is found there.'

A new poem by Khaleed, 'The War is Coming', is about as close to an op-ed as one can get in poetry. It's important to remember that this poem, written in the voice of a Syrian refugee even before it is translated, is already a translation. The Greek text is presented as if it were written in Arabic, and it includes an Arabic phrase. As the epigraph states, it is for the poet Ghayath al-Madhoun as well as the million other Arab poets he stands with. The migrant perspective is slowly introduced to the reader, as the poem gets angrier and angrier. The irony, too, gets thicker until, near the end, we read this over-the-top apology:

I, Ahmed, son of Aisha, although nothing more than a humble migrant, wish to apologize on behalf of the Syrians to Greek men and women for filling their televisions with our deaths as they eat their dinners and wait for their favorite shows, I wish to apologise to the municipal authorities for leaving our trash on their beaches and polluting their shores with tons of plastic, we are uncivilized and we have no environmental awareness, I wish to apologize to the hotel owners and tour operators for damaging the island tourist industry, I wish to apologize for shattering the stereotype of the miserable migrant with our mobile phones and clean clothes, I wish to apologize to the coast guard who have the thankless task of sinking our boats, to the police for standing in disorderly lines, to the bus drivers who have to wear surgical masks to protect themselves from the diseases we carry, I also wish to make a most humble apology to Greek society for exceeding the capacity of their detention camps and for sleeping in their squares and parks – finally, I wish to apologize to the Greek government who had to request additional funds from the European Union in order to pay the purveyors who stock the detention camps, as well as the bus drivers, the police, the coast guard, the tour operators, the hotel owners, the municipal authorities, and the television stations.

(tr. Karen Van Dyck, in Khaleed 2017)

Is this ungrateful, terribly to the point, or both? What's found in this translation of a translation is that giving and taking are never a clear-cut transaction between the haves and have nots. The point is not whether to help, but how. The point is not whether to translate, but how, when, where and what. Always it involves letting go of one kind of life for another. Sometimes the interpretive move hinges on form, sometimes on register or genre, while at other times the venue means everything. I tried to publish this translation in liberal and left-leaning publications in the United States like *The New York Review of Books*, *Harper's*, and *The Nation*, but it was repeatedly rejected. At least one editor was explicit about the reason: it was deemed 'too political'. I finally tried an online literary forum, *Asymptote*, and was happily surprised when the editors ran it in their Translation Tuesday column at *The Guardian*, thus bringing it to a dual audience, readers of poetry and of journalism, and showing that poetry in translation can bridge the distance of what is hard to grasp.

The poets and translators collected in *Austerity Measures* give us a Greece that is as much inside as outside through poems that are as much translations as they are poems. The cross-fertilisation between here and there, at the level of geopolitics and literary categories, is abundantly clear in the last poem of the anthology, Hiva Panahi's 'Ash Person'. The poet adopts the onomatopoetic rhyming of the Greek language after fleeing Kurdistan because it gives her a way to connect her dreams to the present: the first word of the poem, *ta oneira* (dreams), rhymes with the last, *pia* (now). Maria Margaronis's translation makes the connection by beginning and ending with the word 'dreams'. What is and isn't present is hard to fathom when you're on the run, but translation is a place to rest, stop and take account of the new forms of life that letting go of the past makes possible:

Dreams come from far away places
The stones, the birds and I take on new forms of life
Dreams have their own road
And we live far away these days, like dreams.

(p. 415)

WORKS CITED

Katerina Anghelaki-Rooke, *The Scattered Papers of Penelope: New and Selected Poems by Katerina Anghelaki-Rooke*, ed. Karen Van Dyck (Anvil, 2008; Graywolf, 2009).

Theodoros Chiotis, *Futures: Poetry of the Greek Crisis* (Penned in the Margins, 2015).

Nathaniel Davis, ed., *Best European Fiction 2017* (Dalkey Archive, 2016).

Khaleed, Jazra, *Γκρόζνι* (*Grozny*) (Ypokeimeno, 2016).

—, 'The War is Coming', tr. Karen Van Dyck (*The Guarian*: www.goo.gl/78uND4).

Karen Van Dyck, *Austerity Measures: The New Greek Poetry* (Penguin, 2016; NYRB, 2017).

From the Archive

Issue 68, July–August 1989

'Visiting Worser Bay School on Sunday Morning' *by* LAURIS EDMOND

One of Lauris Edmond's ten contributions to the magazine over nine years. Issue 68 also includes Anne Stevenson's 'Letter to Sylvia Plath', six poems by Jonathan Galassi, and John Lee's translations of Perec. David Bellos discusses 'Perec's Puzzling Style' and James Kirkup considers 'Basho's Poetic Thoroughfares'. There are reviews by Clive Wilmer (on Seamus Heaney) and Michael Hamburger (on Idris Parry), among others.

The entire *PN Review* archive, including full PDFs of all 234 issues from 1973 to the present day, is available to subscribers for reading and downloading at www.pnreview.co.uk.

Honeysuckle, taupata, rangiora, briar rose,
the usual Wellington tangle spreading over
the usual hill, steep to the sea; behind me

the school in its soughing pines – and pohutukawas
which also sing to the wind, but not with the aching cry
of the pines. All as it was. Forty years since I

bustled about (I suppose that's what I did)
in these hilltop classrooms, while the amiable
lazy headmaster went off playing golf or bowls.

Hard to believe these moving fictions of time, here
by the sea and the white-shouldered crags, smell
of roots and the salt whiff up from the beach –

even the rebuilt school is the same (there will always
be children). Mine alone is a single season; one spring,
one winter. So. Did I come searching for signs? I see

the years' indifference, prodigal, casual, calm;
the fine ease of growth and decay – and you know
I am oddly released by it. Leaning here, high over

the old tide's patient repetitions, I find myself
smiling and asking, was it forty years, truly,
or four, or – have I forgotten? – four hundred?

Three Poems

MIRIAM NEIGER-FLEISCHMANN

Translated from the Hebrew by Anthony Rudolf & the author

Concept

It feels good
to think of you
as a concept
beyond my reach.

Your physical presence
is hidden
in a projected image.

From now on, I'll love you
only in my secret zone,
only in molecules
with their grains of divinity,

in circular
units of light,
in the pain of your absence.

Objects

The objects in my aunt's house died when she was alive,
since objects come to life with a touch.
For years they were corpses,
while she moved between sofa and couch,
looking at blurred grains
of dust in the air, and the cocoons
of the cockroaches remained after they were sprayed.
When she left for the old people's home
we rescued the objects from their barren existence
and moved them to a rubbish heap for company,
piled high like our guilt feelings for this action,
as heavy as the weight we ascribe to objects
even though they are not our subject of desire.
Now my aunt sits on her bed or in the dining room
with no objective.

My Aunt's House

My aunt and uncle were childless and silent,
always nodding to each other.
The walls of their house were infertile, painted like tapestry,
designed by the flicker of their eyes.
Their memories sat on the table in the living room,
gazing at them like everlasting candles
whose smoke turned what they saw into a daydream.
They did not scream, they had no reason to grumble,
they gave themselves permission to live from one day till the last –
when my uncle moved to the graveyard,
she continued to sit there. She remained silent for him.
And the walls dripped bugs
which fell on her bosom.
And the walls shrank
and pushed her to the old people's home.
A young couple is now living in the house of my aunt
and the walls are pregnant.

Four Poems

PAOLO FEBBRARO

Translated by Adam Elgar

Iscariot

'Why should I talk, when you have said it all
already? Let me take your word for it.
Just as I did when I surrendered, standing
beside him in his followers'
torch-lit circle. It was like sleep,
the first dream of the night. Although the way
he sat disturbed me, with his back so straight,
his voice so light, rigid and gentle
like an absolution. And I found
the fragrance of his miracles smelled dry,
the fringed scroll of the Law. Another – yet
another – priest, and too much poetry.
I leafed more quickly through it all, knowing
how it would end. Both Cup and Cross. When I
embraced his suicide of words, I tore
out of the book the line that most was mine.
I noticed, as I dangled from the tree,
my to-and-fro swing wrote your creaking lines.'

from Suite: August in Ireland

'Don't try anything with me' says the ocean
to the furtive vein of water chiselling itself
into the shore. 'Peat-red, tinted with minerals,
you've no idea of salt's immensity.
Here I have carved a curving bay
where I don't look like me, and where
I let my force out slowly. Look at you
skulking under sand-flattened
bladderwrack, unmade by a bit of sun.
Don't come into my water, don't
try anything with me.' But the stream
has other ideas as it murmurs
cunningly and tries and tries again.

To everyone

And all those who learned Greek on Earth
will find themselves again in Hades
fading with Achilles' shade and living Homer's
incomparable affront to modern faiths.

And Latinists still hypnotised by Virgil's
six-pulsed verses will let Anchises know
what Rome is like, its Fora shoved
aside for churches, and its crooked mayors.

Besotted, credulous Wagnerians
will end up in Walhalla, and among
the lumbering herds of bison, Manito's
celestial prairies will astound sharp-
shooters, tycoons, Wall Street brokers.

As for me, I shall return to these four walls:
fresh tulips by the telephone, a note from you –
'I'm running late' – and in the bedroom
on our still rumpled bed one pillow bears
a hollow hint, and I who slowly notice it
will hope and hope that you don't come.

March has turned...

March has turned so much into river.
The rain has been raising it all month.
I said this yesterday – in silence –
on the bridge, and the convex Tiber
smouldered in its tar
like the vein of a world long gone.

That current wears away the dikes,
it nags them dully, takes their place.
The cruel sun at least allowed contours,
but these have been annexed
by liquid leaving them un-faced.
A seagull like a bomber takes the war
into the air, wipes out in flight,
as one deletes a note,
the liquefying world where it pursues its prey.

Three Poems

IGOR KLIKOVAC

Translated by Igor Klikovac & John McAuliffe

Nettle-Eaters

(Birth of a Language)

Since I first heard about it, I always wanted to see
people eating pain.

Now, as they sit behind the long table, with hands stretched out
onto the white tablecloth, they look like a fed-up delegation,
or an amateur club waiting for the arrival of a grandmaster.

The daydreamy looks show they are reeling in that concentration,
summoning that peace which champions and mass-murderers
walk upon. Whether they'd want to remember or forget something –
who would know, except themselves

but without that, I realise, the whole business is nothing
but a lesson in punctured expectations: noisy, too fast for the eye,
with no revelations or ontological cookie at the end. Something in fact
that pushes itself right out of one's mind

as soon as the waiters start to lift the plastic basins
and uncouple the tables. The green-tongued competitors
exit and belch thunderously in the emptying parking lot.

The Childhood

The hard crust of our city's ice: black engine oil
and crushed kisses on cigarette butts. For a child
that water could remember was entirely logical,
and yet no less magic, and hence full of news about
what was coming. But the landscape remained grey too,
like a spent, badly lit filming location, full of soot
and fooled people, frozen in unwitting pirouettes.

All else was too fast, deceitful or simply mute,
and directed at others. The life trickled into a shallow bowl
and disappeared before lips were brought to it. Only
the discarded and the occasional kindness of weather
could be relied on in the slippery world. Nowadays,
whenever I step into myself through a puddle, I startle,
as I did back then peering over the kitchen sill
each time the winter that stretched between the buildings
got unstitched by the trucks spraying salt.

The River

Standing on the bank I see them pull something black and heavy from the water, and beside a tied sack and a stiff dog unload a puddle with two limp arms and no hands. There is no one in the coat, and workers crouch and lean over the river as if it itself were a question: where is the owner, did he leave the coat before or after? And was he at least a little sorry for the old coat, for the spent life? The river replies with silence, and the coat, the carcass and the secret held by the sack touch each other with profiles, like hieroglyphs. The water could not understand them, so now the hooks, the rain and human horror of dying, negotiate the meaning. Who is who, and what is what in that sentence, which, however things get shuffled, ends in a small death? Like all knots, this one too pushes the handler back, demands retracing of steps, but the semantic needs weight, it always needs some, otherwise it's nonsense or someone else's business, so it's not long before you see it pointing the finger: you're doing your own maths, so chip in, use your own numbers. It's mean of language this, how quickly a word turns personal, more or less as soon as it's abandoned by speech and touched by a thought. Not much time for a pause, just a breath really, and you're not holding an apple in a supermarket, but those Bramleys you jumped fences for as a kid. Clearly, this has its uses, and there's no other way, but still, it's inconsiderate. You don't always want to remember, not every time something's parked in front of your mind... A soaked overcoat and a dead dog? A bloated sack? Of course, right away... The long-lost, forgotten friends and crumbled friendships, a betrayal of trust, a lost love, an unreturned favour, an unresolved dispute, a short shrift, severe consequences, things kept from you, things you kept from others, a slide, a slip, a fall, a splash... The whole sorry shebang, the touched bottom, the slow rot... Or maybe just: faces of the miserable old winos from charity ads.

Underneath the words drying on the deck, the river couldn't be more different. It's steady, uniform and truly endless. It'll show obstinacy or no will at all. It'll be a sharp, pliant metaphor and the most boring thing in the world; annoyingly, sometimes both at the same time. In fact, it'll appear to be so many things that the only safe truth about it will probably be what one sees before any serious thinking has started: water moving from one place to another. With the world beside it, it has a simple contract: it admits only that which has a past that's complete.

A Translation & Three poems

CAROL RUMENS

Cat
freely, after Baudelaire

Come to my warm heart, handsome cat, revise
your nails, soften your feet
and let me drown myself in your handsome eyes,
all metal and agate.

My fingers repeatedly slither
over your head and along your fluent back
till my hand is drunk on your fur
and we *sing the body electric!*

I long for my lover. His stare,
like yours, would be frozen
gunfire.

From head to toe, his air
of pungent, arrogant black man
wrecks me with desire.

A Kandinsky Woodcut

Childishly shapeless in his bell-sleeved nightgown,
one sprite blows a spritely prelude
on a tilted trumpet, pitched
too high for the earthier folk
to catch. But the birch-queen's smiling, she conducts him
with outstretched arms and a length of nonchalant scarf.
Two others dance till their sly, sensual faces
break with the dirty laugh
of a night just around the corner.
In the grass, the copper-plated
leaves are magically turning
to buds of wheat. The birches
stagger on coltish legs, their heads replete
with magpies, Fabergé eggs
and other astonishing brainwaves.

The First-Generation Student & the Secret Scholar

A door swung open on the space where
'university' met 'corporation'
in a muted, steely glissando.

I mistook you for somebody else,
nobody else, a stereotype of profit
and benchmark, obol-murky, paper-light.

I'm years and years too late
for thinking through the conundrum
though I've learned that scholarly kindness

may not be a mask, and masks may be worn over kindness.
A sycamore green-shades your window when
I remember you: can thoughts translate into leaves?

The campus is always September-fresh, the doors
admit us without a card. We first-years crowd
the hall with our voices, again and again and never

Concentric Carol

Watered ash-leaves lament: where tree?
  sing holly berries, sing rosehips
    red green green red
     seed seen
    green red red green
  hide cracked lips, hide hollow berries
tree where lament leaves ash watered.

Scattered ash-stems wonder: whose tree?
  sing armistice, sing armaments
    known names last names
     morphine
    dreams seen lost scenes
  hide hanging ropes, hang wreathes of hopes
tree whose wonder stems ash scattered.

'Just saying no'

Beckett's Epistolary Dissidence

DREW MILNE

IN 1982 SAMUEL BECKETT wrote *Catastrophe* for the Association International de Défense des Artistes. Dedicated to Václav Havel, then an imprisoned Czechoslovakian dissident, the play was performed in nights of solidarity with Havel, first in Avignon, and subsequently in New York and London. *Catastrophe* and *What Where* mark a widely perceived political turn in Beckett's late plays, reshaping Beckett's apparently apolitical stance as a writer.

The perception of Beckett as an apolitical writer has since given way to more nuanced readings of what might be called Beckett's micro-political stances. Aside from French resistance activities Beckett kept private, Beckett's most public acts of solidarity were with other writers and in resistance to censorship. In the context of the 1980s, however, Beckett's solidarity with Havel could not simply be understood as the defence of another writer. As a dissident critic of Czechoslovakian communism, a defence of Havel's human rights and freedom of expression also appeared anti-communist.

Beckett's published writings could also be described as dissident, but not as explicit criticism of any particular regime, more as a negative no-saying, and a rejection of anything resembling cultural affirmation. Construing Beckett as a dissident writer nevertheless feels superficial. As his late letters reveal,[1] Beckett was a persistent no-sayer, turning down requests and blandishments of various kinds in defence of his work's artistic integrity. As Dan Gunn notes: 'Sorry to disappoint' becomes a formula repeated verbatim as often as sixty times during the years represented here'.

[p. lxxxix] Beckett is capable of more belligerent forms of refusal, but there's also a studied rhetoric of polite modesty in his persistent refusal of public positions. In 1968 he writes to Enid Starkie turning down the Oxford Chair of Poetry: 'it is a sorry acknowledgement to have to reply, as I must, no to everything'. [p. 130]

The shortest letter in the collected letters is his refusal to give permission to produce *Eh Joe* with the recorded voice of the actor. Beckett writes, bluntly: 'No' and signs himself 'SB'. [p. 504] Four characters suffice. The gentle denials of influence or relevance with which he responds to critical essays on his work are more elaborate. One gem of polite difference-taking is a letter from 1975: 'Greatly impressed by your erudition & semiotic pyrotechnics. You do me more than proud. Had I had, in my head, when writing in haste that piece, a tenth of what you find, I would deplore it less today.' [p. 410] *Had I had* spins the tense construction. Once unravelled, the implicit correction displaces erudition as the critic's own performance, no reflection of Beckett's labour, and scarcely even merited by the text in question.

Such gestures are rather arch, perhaps, but assimilable within a modesty trope that flatters the poor critic while absenting any authorial approval or responsibility for said critic's criticism. This no-saying is a repetitive feature of Beckett's responses to admiring critics. Beckett's opposition to requests to adapt his works often more directly assert the moral rights of the author not to be messed with. In both modes, Beckett writes to defend his work. The question, then, running through the last volume of his letters is how far Beckett's engaging defence of his writing's aesthetic autonomy is complicit with, or critical of, the political conditions that constrain that autonomy.

Where, for example, did Beckett stand on the Vietnam War? In a letter of March 1968, he writes to Kay Boyle: 'I am grieved to hear of all this incarceration. If you must you must but I wish you'd call it a day and do it all with your pen.' [p.112] Boyle had been imprisoned for demonstrating against the drafting of soldiers into the Vietnam war. Worrying about a friend in peril and hoping that they stay out of prison makes humane sense. But does the advice 'do it all with your pen' constitute a critique of political demonstrations?

To what extent did Beckett offer a critique of the Vietnam War with his own pen? Beckett's broad political sympathies are not in doubt: 'Is Nixon the only hope? Jesus!' [p. 112] Although his letters scarcely ever develop a political critique of unfolding events, such events are nevertheless glimpsed. In another letter from 1968, Beckett writes of 'Awful stuff from Genet'. [p. 138]. The reference is to Jean Genet's essay accusing the American public of blindness to atrocities in Vietnam. The turn of phrase – 'awful stuff' – is knowingly compressed and ambiguous, leaving it open whether Genet's essay is awful as writing or whether it is the politics and atrocities represented by Genet that are awful. Perhaps both.

There is a similar question of tone and complicity in Beckett's brief references to the Paris uprisings of 1968, which take place more or less right outside Beckett's apartment. In a rather oblique letter to Theodor Adorno, Beckett writes: 'I have not yet been conspué, so far as I know and that is not far, by the Marcusejugend. As you said to me once at the Iles Marquises, all is malentendu. Was ever such rightness joined to such foolishness?' [p.151] Adorno had his own difficulties with student radicals, but the phrase 'Marcusejugend' is strangely coded and barbed, perhaps within an in-joke with Adorno that references some shared conversational wit.

The conjunction of rightness with foolishness appears wearily damning of the aspirations of the student uprising. Such witty but rather darkly sarcastic detachment also features in a letter Beckett writes to Ruby Cohn amidst May '68: 'This on fringe of pop rioting. All quiet now. Dream university on its way.' [p. 130]. The editors offer a heroic gloss on pop rioting as a Gallicism, but the phrase also carries with it a touch of ironic contempt for the concept of pop and for aspirations towards a better higher education system.

Beckett's world-weary epistolary style perhaps forces him into this kind of ironic and witty relation to contemporary events, but the irony comes at the expense of earnest intent. He informs Barbara Bray, for example, that he has been reading Edmund Wilson's *To the Finland Station* 'with as much interest as I can muster for such vital matters'. [p. 282] 'Vital matters', like 'awful stuff', cuts two ways. Assessing the vitality of *To the Finland Station* for Beckett's own thinking is not helped by the further remark to Bray quoted in Dan Gunn's introduction: 'hate myself now even more while less Marxist-Leninist than ever'. [p. lxxxi]. Lessness, as Beckett often avers, does not constitute some necessary dialectical difference. Less

Marxist-Leninist need not mean more right-wing, but it is surprising that Beckett ever assessed his distance from Marxist-Leninism, and puzzling that he should hate himself the more in such assessment. Presumably the wit here amounts to ironic self-mockery for the helplessness of his lack of political commitment.

The pithy imploding negativity that makes so many of his letters entertaining to read also disables anything so extended as a political argument. One of Beckett's most surprising political one-liners emerges in a discussion of the German translation of *Not I*: 'Does the lack of present participles explain Hitler? Nothing to tell.' [p. 329] That there might be a powerful politics at play in grammatical differences between languages is quickly despatched into the no to everything that accompanies anything resembling argument. Beckett was evidently speculating on the political entailments of grammatical orthodoxy, but has little to say by way of argued narrative. The dynamics of Beckett's performance can be read by analogy through Hegel's critique of the beautiful soul. Beckett even appears to be more interested in chess and rugby than the fate of Paris in '68, Vietnam or the economic and political crises of the 1970s and 1980s.

Reading through the late letters does not provide much new information on Beckett's construction of himself as a writer working at a marked distance from political engagement. In his acts of micro-solidarity with Eastern European writers and translators, there's scarcely a sense that Beckett wants to address his complicity with the cold war. But even as late in Beckett's life as 1987, the evidence is contradictory. Writing to James Knowlson, amid plans to set up an advisory board for the Beckett International Foundation Trust, Beckett takes against the suggestion that the French Minister of Culture, Jack Lang, might be a member. He writes: 'Don't much like thought of Lang as patron & political whiff we were better without' [p. 690]. Keeping the integrity of his literary work free of 'political whiffs' appears to be a persistent orientation through his working life.

Beckett is nevertheless capable of surprising acts of explicit political affiliation. Also in 1987, Beckett writes to Israel Halperin: 'You may count on me among the supporters of your Chile campaign and add my name to the list of signatories.' [p. 691] Signing up to the campaign against human rights abuses in Chile is perhaps, for Beckett, a moral or humane action rather than a political gesture, but this certainly has a political whiff. What is perhaps more striking, however, is the way Beckett's letter to Halperin is direct, unironic and lacking in his characteristic wit, as if in recognition that ironic wiggle room is evasive rather than witty when signing a collective political statement.

More characteristic of Beckett's epistolary wit is autocritical negativity, a negativity that seeks to squeeze some life out of every flat phrase and dead metaphor. It is as if being found in possession of a linguistic habit were the deeper political sin:

Even for space-gazing, no zest left. It's wholly ghost I'll be soon. No less than all the dear departed. Without their advantages. Keep dropping us the odd line, awhiff with the old wit, before we give it up. [p. 632]

Better, it seems, to be awhiff with the old wit than suffer some political whiff.

For all that Beckett's epistolary style seeks to avoid being found clichéd, the closer the style engages with explicit public statement, or statements that stand outside informal dialogue, the closer the writing comes to polite statements of gratitude, respect and consolation. In letters of friendship and solidarity, Beckett abandons his characteristic twists of grammatical convention and semantic negativity, and offers a humanist sincerity his writing otherwise mocks. This is perhaps most evident in Beckett's letter to Václav Havel: 'To have helped you, however little, and saluted you and all you stand for, was a moment in my writing life that I cherish. It is I who stand in your debt.' [p. 614] Beckett elsewhere mocks conceptions of the writer's writing life, his own especially. There is something puzzling, then, about Beckett saluting Havel not just as a fellow writer, but all that he stands for, although 'stands for' has some of the compressed ambiguity of 'awful stuff' and 'vital matters'.

Havel's famous essay on 'the power of the powerless' suggests a mode of critical dissidence that Beckett might have found richly suggestive, but there is scarce evidence that Beckett ever engaged with what Havel stood for, beyond his status as playwright. Indeed, it is difficult to make sense of Beckett's stated support for Havel amid the absence of political co-ordinates that characterises Beckett's letters. Beckett may have supported a prominent Eastern European dissident, but his own epistolary dissidence is much more evident in the restless negativity of his less public forms of wit and repartee.

1 *The Letters of Samuel Beckett*, volume 4: 1966–1989, eds. George Craig, Martha Dow Fehsenfeld, Dan Gunn & Lois More Overbeck (Cambridge: Cambridge University Press, 2016).

Two Poems

JACK HANSON

Mere Semblance

Something within me, friend,
is not my own.

The angle of the ridge
is hard as steel

and cuts the sky in two.
I was once like

that ridge and before then,
pre-severed sky:

shapeless in form, filled out
with white purple.

And then I was graceful
and it was good

to see you. And as if
I had never

been, there's now another
who dwells within

and whom one sees like glass,
there and not there,

a semblance of space
dividing things up.

Somehow in C Major

Put on some Schubert
and that was the end.
The leaves, some affixed
to their spindly stems,
all came tumbling
down like a vicious
snow. The arrogance,
that I could have felt,
that I could have loved
enough to keep out
death, your death (now 'hers',
since all our talking
is over with). Soul-
affirming, though, all
of this is. My heart
creaks at the weight, like
the door of a safe,
or her old chair. Five
strings plucked and pulled seem
to say this, perhaps
something greater. Some
indication, then,
that even around
the corner, we might
continue to turn.

Switchblade

JAY DEGENHARDT

– Klytaimestra does not know what light is. She does not know about wavelengths and spectra and optic nerves.
– She does know the shape dark cuts around it.
– *Kolpos* means 'bosom, lap, womb; fold formed by a loose garment; any hollow'.
– Klytaimestra was afraid of the dark as a child.
– Klytaimestra had two brothers.
– Notes on Klytaimestra are highlighted in red or purple.
– When Klytaimestra goes to bed she rocks her ankles as though to throw off the day's stasis. Her husband does not notice this but has learnt to let it soothe him to sleep. Klytaimestra's lover finds it endearing and kisses the bone joint that juts out above her heel.
– This bone is called the talus and is used to make dice.
– While away at war Klytaimestra's husband can't sleep. Sometimes the shaking of his mistress is enough.
– Notes on Kassandra are highlighted in black.
– Klytaimestra uses the word 'affect' as a noun but her daughter tries to correct her.
– 'A Greek woman's dress (*peplos*) was somewhere between a tunic and a mantle, with plenty of extra fabric in the upper part in which to carry a baby, or to draw over the head or before the eyes.'
– One night is filled with clouds and Klytaimestra is not ready to go to bed. She moves downstairs and onto the grey tiles of the porch. She sees a light.
– The crime Klytaimestra is most likely to commit is martyrdom.
– The light is the glint of a knife's edge. It is Iphigenia turning over her switchblade. It was a gift from her father. Klytaimestra approaches from behind and seizes her daughter's hand. She coils Iphigenia's fingers over the edge until red seeps out from the palm. She says her lifeline was too short and she will carve it longer.
– The crime Klytaimestra is most likely to be tried for is sabotage.
– Her husband is an open (unsheathed) blade.
– Klytaimestra is not an open (unsheathed) blade.

Four Poems

JOHN UPTON

Scream

It made no sense, but perfect sense. As lovers
they'd revelled – theatre, concerts, galleries.
Now she screamed, 'Get out of the car! Get out!'
She was order, control, controlling, fashionable,
dressing up for theatre. He was orderly
but out of order, careless, dressing down
in jeans and two-or-three-day clothes. Love's magic
seventy and tragic thirty percent.
Now, as she drove the car –
out of nothing, really, but everything –
she disdaining his opinion of the play they'd seen,
he objected to her tone, her character.
She hit the brakes then, screaming,
ordered him out. He looked at where they were:
down by the docks at midnight, lifeless streets,
a desolated landscape. Hours passed
in seconds. He stayed silent. Silently
she drove him to his car. They realised
this was the end. Alone and driving home
he knew, and knew she knew,
only two people still in love would fight like that.

Navigation

You see the light, you navigate the wide
welcoming entrance to the dark complexity
of love in the lit carpark, you park beneath
the neon in the numbered space your husband
has given you, divorce is under way
as for you both it simply wasn't working,
and yet as you point and ping to lock the car
that same ping seems to catch your heart, aware
of love in a letting go that will be gathered up
again, you know it's hopeless, and perhaps
this is the last time,
but once again, for an hour, your heart
is feathery, you're a teenager, a bride,
walking the numbers on these doors, you're caught
in a love that lifts you up, you know
your landing wheels are permanently down now
but it doesn't matter, this hour perhaps will stretch
to two, it's an oasis from adjustment,
and if you cry at midnight they'll be earned tears
and somehow worth residual aching for
this sweetness, or so it seems right now as
you find the numbered door, you've seen
his car, he's in here, and you love him
as much as ever now the loss is definite,
and he needs you as much, just for this hour,
and then you'll come apart, adjust your clothes
and leave, your broken hearts relieved, committed
to the abyss, beyond an isolated
world of passion in a little room,
two lovers who each know the other's body
with certainty, without embarrassment.
You have the key, you're turning it.

Heart of Glass

She loves her work, she is her work. For twenty years
she does it well, and then her manager
calls her in. The HR personnel
are there, they're never there. He says,
We're cutting costs.
She wishes in that disembodied way
she wasn't here in this high-viz environment,
glass walls, she wishes she was in
the toilets throwing up. The
world is glass, she's glass, blown and transparent,
breakable, but she's like those robots making cars,
as well, on auto. *There'll be a package.* She
signs the paper, she's at the hospital
when she had the miscarriage and grief moved in
like a lodger, and her husband couldn't cope.
You'll finish up this afternoon.
She goes to her desk and she's a box, a box
with a heavy hasp and a padlock through the eye,
a box of shards, of broken glass, the miniature
shattered toys of childhood – small and delicate
figurines, the cutting edges begging
for fingers, blood. Clearing her desk, she watches
from across the street, she watches through the walls.
HR say something, promising
references, three weeks retraining, at fifty-one
her best days are ahead. At home her husband
is living in his box, making his cars.

The Duchess of Malfi Never Stood a Chance

The seagulls float like paper or walk in white
shirts and grey waistcoats on the esplanade
as she flies from her balcony twenty storeys up.
Birds promenade past tables on the quay
as she drops. Their feet and beaks, a red ensemble,
match her expensive shoes, the left of which
is now detaching.

Just an hour ago, she and her brother
sat at an outdoor table. As she stared
at her chocolate-stained cappuccino he said,
The Duchess of Malfi was staged in Shakespeare's theatre.
It seems that family problems never change.
Using both hands, she raised her cup and sipped.
She grew a moustache, he brushed his lip and smiled.
She brushed her lip. Two seagulls were taking off
their waistcoats for a fight, or perhaps it was sex.
They skittered and jumped. Sipping again, she wondered
why he'd invited her to this play, in which
two brothers kill their sister, who has taken
a lover, brought dishonour to the family.
Putting down her cup, afraid of certainty,
she said, 'You're looking sad.' 'I am,' he told her.

Red feet are dancing on the esplanade
then suddenly the seagulls leap and fly.

'A sad and angry consolation'

Yeats, Landor, Hill & An Unwritten Book

PETER MCDONALD

WHEN WE THINK ABOUT the recently dead, there is often regret about what we failed to say to them, and about the conversations we never got around to having. But at the service in Oxford in October 2016 in memory of Geoffrey Hill, my own thoughts wandered towards the things I had never managed to write – such thoughts being (I knew) singularly inappropriate to the occasion.

In the early 2000s, when I first (and very fearfully) started to be in regular contact with Hill, I felt that I might be making a start on a new book, one about anger in literature. It would be about dramatic anger, in the unstable reactor cores for the nuclear power of plays like *King Lear* and *Othello*; about the uncontrollable and yet somehow controlled and directed anger in Dryden, in Swift and in Pope; and about the slow diminution of authorial anger in poetry from the nineteenth century onwards, to the point where it had become one of the least respectable of emotions in any self-respecting work. I never wrote the book, and one of the many reasons for this failure was that I had become too caught up in my own subject – too angry about too much – with the result that I was unable to work through the topic of anger in any useful way. I thought then (and, in a way, think now) that it might have been a good book, but I was no longer the person to write it – if indeed I had ever been.

There was another, much less personal, problem with the outline of this project: in common with a number of other big critical ideas, the flaw in its argument came with a name attached – that of W. B. Yeats. For Yeats, as I had known all along, wasn't in the least embarrassed by instances of anger in his poetry, let alone in his other writing and his public behaviour. The temper of a poem like 'Parnell's Funeral' is not that of a man who wants to be liked ('Come, fix upon me that accusing eye. / I thirst for accusation.') Arch-networker that he remained from youth to age, Yeats was good neither with crowds nor in them; he knowingly and persistently gave offence, and he understood the centrality of anger (his own, and others') to his own artistic power. I reflected on the fact that this foremost modern poet had also been the angriest, and reminded myself of how deeply resonant I had always found his lines in 'A Dialogue of Self and Soul'; from the first time they possessed me in my late teens, they had seemed to map out my own life of writing and thinking about poetry:

What matter if I live it all once more?
Endure that toil of growing up;
The ignominy of boyhood; the distress
Of boyhood changing into man;
The unfinished man and his pain
Brought face to face with his own clumsiness;

The finished man among his enemies? –
How in the name of Heaven can he escape
That defiling and disfigured shape
The mirror of malicious eyes
Casts upon his eyes until at last
He thinks that shape must be his shape?

I was always astonished – I remain astonished – by the way in which that expostulation of irritated impatience ('How in the name of Heaven') is so perfectly caught and kept in balance by Yeats's verse here: technically and imaginatively (these being somehow the same), the line is a small miracle. But the path that is charted is hardly a reassuring one. At all events, it didn't reassure me, and I came to understand that a book about literary anger would end up being a book about Yeats, even a defence of him, which would force me into a confrontation with my own image in many sets of 'malicious eyes'.

There were other poets besides Yeats who would have holed my argument in such a book below the waterline. The first of these was W. S. Landor, greatly prolific and greatly angry, who had cut a bad-tempered swathe through much of the literary nineteenth century, and had (amongst other things) provided Robert Browning with some of the raw materials for his skilfully transposed and modulated uses of anger in semi-dramatic poetic contexts. Between 2000 and 2005 I read, if not all, then most of Landor; enough, anyway, to become mildly obsessed with him: he was not a great poet, like Yeats, but a real one nonetheless, and a writer of prose whose sometimes slippery eloquence protected a hard centre of principled and spikily independent thought. If Landor's art had been stiffened and strengthened by anger, his life had been largely ruined by the same ungoverned emotion. I had no moral points to make about any of this – Landor's life had been his to ruin as he saw fit – but I did feel myself drawing closer and closer to the sparking current of Landor's scorn for, frustration with, and fury about his times. My times, I knew, were different ones; but they were scarcely better. I found my own dislike of a few contemporary critics and poets being shaped (tainted, maybe) by Landor's intensity of anger from a century and a half before. I acted nowhere near as violently or outspokenly as he habitually did, confining myself to the publication (not even, in fact, the writing) of a few strongly negative critical reviews; but in short order letters were being sent to my employers to demand my immediate dismissal in the name of contemporary decency; poets were threatening to sue for six-figure sums for the indignity of having their verses called bad; and wild libels were being sprayed in my direction from offended publishers and writers. One such attack was even praised in the papers by the then Poet Laureate. Somehow or other, as it struck me, Landor seemed to have been involved in the whole row. Again, this figure who demanded a place in my argument was a dangerous one to handle, and he was able (or so I thought) to cause me plenty of trouble from beyond the grave. I had to walk away, from Landor and from the feuds of my own making.

Another poetic figure helped to put any plans for a book on anger to rest, and this was Geoffrey Hill. Here, in truth, the poet might have worked rather well as a clinching case for the general contention that anger as such had become unacceptable; for, strange as this must now seem, in the early 2000s Hill was still accounted unsuitable in the world of contemporary poetry. There was always a lot that the literary establishment held against Hill; but at that time – the time following the publication of books such as *The Triumph of Love* and *Speech! Speech!* – anger was certainly one count on which his work was generally held to be guilty. And of course that poetry, or a lot of it, was indeed the poetry of anger. There was – as I suppose there always is – a lot to be angry about, and the Hill of the first decade of the twenty-first century articulated a fury about the major outrages, injustices, and impertinences of a wretched time which was compounded with the frankly personal, and even the self-consciously petty. For many reviewers, and for all the prize-juries busy about their perennial task of rewarding the worthy for their worthiness, this was altogether bad form. There was an uncomfortable awareness that Hill might not actually *like* the reviewers and the jurors, the poetry-tipsters and the *zeitgeist*-watchers, very much at all; and nobody in those circles likes any poetry without the reassurance that the poetry likes them back.

As I sat through the memorial service, those days seemed very far away. Oxford was doing what it does best and celebrating the eminence of the eminent; and there was a general air of enlightened magnanimity about the finely-managed proceedings, in which Hill's last years, when he was the University's Professor of Poetry, were especially prized. Those years – and those lectures – are certainly worth celebrating. In the privacy of my thoughts, though, I could feel some troubling presences: the memory of my hour-long conversation with Geoffrey, when I persuaded him to stand for that post, and his frankness about his feelings of dread when he thought of what might be expected of him in it; and the uneasiness, sometimes expressed as open scorn, among eminent Oxford figures (some of them now busy celebrating him) at the time his candidacy was mooted; then the poet's own voice, with its part-theatrical intonation, saying to me with deadly emphasis, 'They will *loathe* you for it, and they already hate you for being associated with Hill.' Unwelcome presences, all of these memories: minor ones, mired in their pointless and now slightly ridiculous anger. Yet I knew that Hill, who had an uneasy stand-off for most of his life with Yeats, was profoundly alert to what was involved in having to behold his own image in 'the mirror of malicious eyes' and that, like Yeats, he was an artist with enough power to see more than just the things presented to him in that glass. Thus comforted, I was able to listen with a measure of philosophical tolerance to a further Oxonian eulogy, which praised especially Hill's habit of joking about himself in his

lectures. Only Oxford, after all, would still measure a man's worth by his capacity for self-deprecation.

In the midst of the service, it struck me that I had lost the knack of anger. Those things that used to enrage me now saddened me – hurt me, indeed – but they no longer provoked me into risking far too much with far too little real strength to back it up. The best artists – artists like Yeats and Shakespeare, like Pope and Swift, and like Hill – had the ability to harness anger in their art; while the lesser artists – and certainly the lesser lesser artists like me – could only be destroyed by anger's force, doomed to see themselves as they were seen in the angry eyes of others, and to act accordingly.

Right at the close of the Oxford service, and as a potent contrast to the beautiful but solemn music that had been performed throughout, a guitarist and a banjo-player saw us out to jaunty, half-plaintive, sad-happy bluegrass. As I looked back at the door, there they still were, filling the enormous and now almost empty chapel of Keble College with that lovely, lonely sound. Some phrases, not of Hill's but of Yeats's, also echoed through my head. One – attuned to Oxford and to my own mixed feelings about Oxford and Geoffrey Hill – was the splendidly double line, 'The finished man among his enemies.' Another – intended to be sung drunkenly to the memory of Parnell, and never likely to feature in any future University mission-statements – was the line 'a proud man's a lovely man': it is true to Geoffrey, and to my memory of him. One above all, though, answered more exactly to the occasion, and to the jingling echoes of the hillbilly music: it was that electric conjunction of words in the phrase 'tragic joy'. Very quickly, one should say (and I could almost hear Hill mordantly making this point), Yeats dishonoured his own genius by treating the phrase as a mere slogan. Nevertheless, in the hands of the very greatest artists, anger can be transfused and transfigured into this, or something like this. Nobody needs a book to offer its explanation of the process. And a book wouldn't help; for only art does that. I had lines from *The Triumph of Love* by heart, and I heard them all the way home:

So – Croker, MacSikker, O'Shem – I ask you:
what are poems for? They are to console us
with their own gift, which is like perfect pitch.
Let us commit that to our dust. What
ought a poem to be? Answer, *a sad
and angry consolation*. What is
the poem? What figures? Say,
a sad and angry consolation. That's
beautiful. Once more? A *sad and angry
consolation*.

(*The Triumph of Love*, CXLVIII)

Two Poems

ADAM THORPE

Mud Puddle

1

There is thought down there, or even
conjecture. An appetite like a famished pike's.

My grandfather's *Classical Myth and Legend*
would fall open to Hylas, as painted by Waterhouse,

still among the living on the water's edge,
precariously leaning with his shiny jug

towards a pubescent flotilla of girls,
their long hair dark as the pond's sludge.

He was me, baffled at the age of twelve.
Nipple-deprived, albino-white, with succulent,

vermilion lips, it was only their desire
that made them desirable. I wanted to be

lord of the underwater gloom, spoilt silly,
wrapped in their waist-length russet hair

like the clammy entanglements of *Myriophyllum
spicatum*, laughing open-mouthed without

the bubbles of air. A treasured trophy,
hidden from my family under lily pads.

2

The summer has been dry: already the levels
are descending, the inlets showing their ribbed

banks, like a tyre's treads. At my next school
there is to be a legendary place –

a high-roofed skylight over the girls' showers
that some will crawl to, always

disappointed by the steam's mist,
that blur of condensation as the hot pipes

ring beneath them, voyeur-defying. It will
always be like this, with nothing to see

bar one's own face, like an ugly Narcissus
dreaming of nymphs, devising that other myth.

Then

The cottage hush was neither of us at work
in the days before mobiles, kids, computers.
Only the odd squeak of the public phone box
bang in front, its muffled tender of chat
and goster, an occasional episode of shrieks.

I'd tilt at something like *Don Quixote*
or scribble verse upstairs in thick socks
as you knitted that jumper over Plath's *Letters*.
We slept till eleven, went for mud-loud hikes.
The bucket accumulated a timpani of leaks

while the coal-fire shoved into the narrow room
in sour puffs, encouraged by certain winds
over the moors. My father had left the village
(born and bred here, the cottage his *pied à terre*)
at sixteen. The war! What must that mean, to be born

and bred in the same place? I had no idea.
He'd raised his hand when the colonel came, college
swapped for a uniform and the deaths of friends.
I'd wafted through life and was wafting on, foam
on a privileged wave. We'd sortie out to the 'Green'

or 'The Miner's Standard' up on the brow, see
the locals who'd known him, like Eric, whose stories
I'd record over hours and hours on cassette.
Tales from the Peaks! 'He were away a bit,
your dad,' said Eric. 'But now he's back.' Over thirty

years! 'Ey up, you forget. Feels like ten.
En't nowt, that.' A lot of frosts on the slate,
of summers not giving a hand with the hay. Time varies
for no one, and although there's nowhere for me to be
away from like him, another thirty's gone since then.

Two Poems

BECKY CULLEN

Opening

My shoes come sleeping in a box.
I hear them breathe inside their tissue-paper book,
the sound of rippling leaves.

The sole is thick alright, like a slab of black tripe;
the toes are tapered and stopped inside,
adding another inch, at least, in length.

Who knows I spade my feet? Kick trees
until the bark flakes, then blame the deer?
Who knows I use my shoes to root?

These are wild shoes
with points like noses, keen like foxes,
the leather creased like ears.

Mother

Sometimes she is sick with new children, sometimes she is heavy with old ones.
Panels hide cupboards stuffed with capes and muffs, stacks of dove-grey boxes.
Panels hide balding dolls with wrists and ankles creased and fat. In a box,
there are boots with wooden soles for babies. There are boots for babies,
with wooden soles. The walls whisper things and promise. Her hands lie loose
in her lap. Lace droops on her arm. Her door is closed to queues of questions.
Her hands lie loose in her lap, when they should be busy blanketing or running.
Her cloth puckers at will, crumples; her palms are too hot, her fingers too heavy.
On the table, a pair of silver bird scissors, a pair of gold-rimmed reading glasses.
There's a border she should be stitching, a border of a blue-winged fledgling.
Her hands lie loose in her lap. She slips out a child every year from under her skirts,
imagines every other baby crumpled in a brown paper bag. The walls whisper things
and promise. There are boots for babies with wooden soles. There's a border
she should be stitching. Her hands lie loose in her lap.

Three Poems

LEO MAYER

The Fathers

Follow now this fold of laundered fathers
fussed-over, discreet, temperate, unrattled.
Skin plays down in mouthfuls, pretty leather
strung fancily and with great care. Settled
children pause, confessing wonder – cars
dispel with motion all the sicknesses

of standing still. At home these fathers doze
or simmer, tend the placid bathwater;
with a practised and digestible ease
express opinion. Their wedded fingers
gently tame the sugary devices
of a threatening yet sweetly toothless

age. What have our fathers brought to bloated
birth if not themselves? So happily
they sway with cargo, proliferate
like missiles. The strictest penalties
would not dissuade them from their growth, for see
how stubbornly they slumber, braced as trees.

Quelques Alexandrines

As in Debussy's *Preludes*: the melodies are
fitted then briskly dismantled; how they trail

filigrees of quickly falling snow... So it is
the leitmotif of fire when your memory
expands in grace or gentleness upon my mind.

The Favourite

Smiles from the esplanade.
Swift gestures signify

a short disquiet, almost
momentary. Some good news

is gathered noisily. He floats
appropriate proposals.

But privately what we would know
of great men often hides

itself away, distributing
considered gifts or alms in lieu

of sympathy. At times it is
a wooden god, deforested

his look, his staff felled slowly.
Its leaf will not put forth.

Edwin Morgan: Translator's Notebook (2)

JAMES McGONIGAL

This piece continues a series started in *PNR* 233 that draws on Edwin Morgan's mainly unpublished writings on translation. Preserved in the Edwin Morgan Papers at the Special Collections in the University of Glasgow Library (UGL), these writings help to reconstitute Morgan's creative thinking in relation to the poetry of other cultures. McGonigal's editing is signalled in the text.

MONTALE WAS AT the forefront of Edwin Morgan's mind in 1956, as a translator and also as a young poet in search of an authentic voice of his own. He would use Montale as an exemplar of his own practice, where he would sometimes encounter in the process of insightful translation a sort of *Ur*-poem which both the translator and the original poet seemed to share. Such 'co-ownership' was doubtless comforting at a time when his own poetry was proceeding slowly, and when journal editors often retained his translations for publication but returned his original poems with regrets. A full statement of this sense of poetic partnership was given on the weekend of 23–26 March 1956, when Morgan chaired a symposium on 'Translation', introducing the session with a detailed paper at the Sixth Annual Conference of Non-professorial University Teachers in the University College of North Staffordshire, Keele (see 'Translator's Notebook' part 1, *PNR* 233).

A glance at the list of holograph poems that he preserved in his Papers for that year (available at www.goo.gl/jouerc) reveals that after the conference he worked on translations of Montale to the exclusion of almost all original work. This focus is recorded from May onwards, sometimes leading to several translations over a two-day period. These would form his first full collection of translations, *Poems from Eugenio Montale* (1959), published by the School of Art at the University of Reading, with the Italian text of twenty-one poems printed with facing translation. But Morgan's Preface to this collection, reprinted in *Collected Translations* [CT], suggests he had already discovered a more personal sense of identification with Montale (as he would also experience with Vladimir Mayakovsky, Sándor Weöres, Attila József and others), and which he came to see as an important factor in effective translation. He would discuss one of his Montale translations towards the end of that year, at a talk he gave in the University of Bristol in December 1956.

Although the holograph translations are all dated after the Keele seminar in March 1956, Morgan included '35 Poems from Eugenio Montale' in a file of typescript translations and dated these 1955–1960 (UGL: MS Morgan E/1/2). So his attraction to Montale must have preceded this talk on translation. Some of these versions did not appear in *Poems from Eugenio Montale*, and remain uncollected. Their overall sense of a stoical isolation, longing, and threat might suggest that in part Morgan was finding in Montale's hermetic work echoes of his own fraught life as a gay man in Scotland's dark and disapproving 1950s. The following unpublished translation from *Ossi di Seppia* shows Morgan's determination to reflect the form and tenor of the original. Yet it also seems to evoke an uneasy underworld that culminates in a shuddering realisation of dangers run.

MERIGGIARE PALLIDO E ASSORTO

Dozing at midday, dazed and pale,
Beside a scorching orchard wall,
Hearing the twigs and dry scrub make
A crack for the blackbird, a rustle for the snake:

Spying on the ants in their red processions
Over the tares or in wrinkles of ground,
Now breaking file and now in collision
At the summit of some tiny mound:

Watching far down through the leaves
The shimmering scales of the sea-waves
While shrill cicadas send their cries
Quivering up from grassless crags:

And feeling with an unhappy wonder
In the dazzling sunlight where you've sauntered
That life and everything it labours under
Is there in that wall you followed, with a shudder
Looking up where its sharp broken bottles are flaunted!

It was the work of translation in the previous year of 1955, then, which contributed to the confident internationalism with which Morgan now spoke to his academic peers at Keele and Bristol. Adding to his earlier extended translation experience with Old English in *Beowulf* and other shorter poems (CT: 245–55), and the Renaissance love lyrics of Maurice Scève (CT: 166–76) which he began while completing his undergraduate studies after war service, he had now consolidated his skills in Italian and French translation and expanded the range eastwards. Here are his chosen poets of 1955, with the month in which he translated them:

January: Théophile de Viau and Torquato Tasso. *February*: Giambattista Marino. *March–April*: St-Amant. *April*: Pablo Neruda. *July*: Aleksandr Pushkin, Mikhail Lermontov, Yekaterina Shevelyova and Lesya Ukrainka. *July–August*: Taras Shevchenko (the last two poets named being Ukrainian). *August*: Vera Inber. *September*: Boris Pasternak and Anna Akhmatova. *November*: Lesya Ukrainka. *December*: Giacomo Leopardi.

The month of May appears to be missing from the list, but was the most memorable time of all. This was when Morgan took part in a month's study tour of Russia, organised by the Scotland-USSR Friendship Society, which took him and a small party of teachers and journalists to Moscow, Leningrad and

Kiev, visiting universities, ballet and theatre, collective farms, an orphanage, various ministries, galleries and museums. He documented the trip in great detail in two small notebooks, and collected tickets, programmes, postcards, prices of shop goods, notes of student numbers and curricula as aides-memoire (UGL: MS Morgan H/1/1). Thus in his comment on Russian literature textbooks in the lecture at Keele, he spoke from recent experience.

May Day fell on a Sunday that year, and at the official celebration in Red Square he was introduced to Yekaterina Shevelyova, 'poetess and journalist', who spoke English and French. Morgan read from his Mayakovsky translations and from his *Beowulf* in the Hand and Flower Press edition (1952), and she read from her own work. All this took place against a background of 'relentless' military music. He presented her with a copy of *Beowulf* and some issues of the Scottish poetry journal *Lines Review*. She presented him with a copy of her latest volume of poetry, and they arranged to meet again for further discussion.

On a later visit to the Ministry of Social Security he was seated beside Shevelyova, and they had time to discuss modern poetry (Eliot, Pound and, her favourite, Dorothy Parker) and her impressions of Scottish poetry in *Lines Review*. She had found it difficult, especially Hugh MacDiarmid, but undertook to translate some shorter pieces. Morgan quizzed her on Mayakovsky's continuing influence, which she claimed still to detect, even in a decade more influenced by socialist realism, as a counterpoint to the regularity of contemporary rhythms. She admired Konstantin Simonov (three-times winner of the Stalin Prize), but also Vera Inber and Boris Pasternak, with reservations. In her view, hard work in poetry was more important than inspiration, but she stressed the centrality of imagination.

It is hard to judge from his notebook record exactly what Morgan made of all this, but on his return to Scotland he translated some of her poems and wrote a piece about the 'Soviet poetess' entitled 'Communicators' for *Saltire Review* (II:6, Winter 1955: pp. 66–9). Here he describes her work as 'genuine minor poetry', representative of poetic themes and ideas in contemporary Russia: 'The style tends to be declamatory, ringing and clear; and the subjects tend to come from the life of the moment, with little interposition of symbol or fable. For this poetry, it can be said that it is seldom obscure; against it, that it is seldom profound.' In response to his questions about the recent Russian poetry's unsurprising imagery, its absence of verbal or sonic surprise and its repetitious subject matter (Stalin, the Volga-Don Canal, Korea), she had replied that since the revolutionary days of Blok and Mayakovsky were over, socialist realism and 'the need to communicate' were more important than dazzling metaphors and new forms. To Morgan's query as to whether this might result in injustice to a more subtle and difficult poet like Pasternak, who seemed under-represented in Soviet anthologies, Shevolyova's answer 'combined a fellow-poet's admiration for Pasternak's great art and talent with a good Soviet citizen's distrust of his complexity. [...] "Often you can't find your way about because of the *sound* of his poems!".'

Morgan noted the presence of women among the celebrated names of current Russian poetry (he mentions Margarita Aliger and Vera Inber as well as Shevelyova), and had asked about the predominance of public as against personal themes in their work. A subordination of the personal to the political is recognised, and the pressure of public expectation during a period of post-war reconstruction. But he preferred a poetry 'where the personal and the public were successfully intermingled'.

His work of translation of contemporary Russian poets certainly intensified on his return to Scotland. This included 'The Pulkova Meridian' (1943) by Vera Inber (CT: 405–6) and works by Pasternak that would appear in Morgan's *Sovpoems* collection from Migrant Press (1961), alongside translations from Mayakovsky, Tsvetayeva, Tikhonov, Martynov and Yevtushenko (CT: 27–55, again with a substantial Preface). Uncollected but also of interest are several of Shevelyova's poems published in the *Saltire Review* article, with a socialist perspective which Morgan shared, and the memory of a wartime partnership which he did not want to let go.

Here is one he describes as having 'a double moral', where the 'solidarity and unity of purpose seen in the V-shaped flight of the cranes are transferred to the action and life of Russia as a whole', with this truth about self-discipline being addressed especially to the next generation being educated in Soviet schools:

THE CRANES

They stood there, a grizzled old man
And a schoolboy, looking out over
The harvested fields at the sky,
At a far-off triangle of cranes
Flying from the land.

Neither sea, hill nor plain
Nor dazing lightning can ever
To the united be snare or scare
Or unweld the wedge they range
Through the free air and

Nothing will cause them to turn
From their aim as they wing after
The one that leads them. – It is clear
That far flights, birds' or brains',
Like geometry demand

Disciplined hands!

In Morgan's favourite of her poems, where a political educator visits a Moscow household on a cold night, he finds 'a current of genuine imaginative feeling which saves it from being sentimental or pretentious':

FEBRUARY 1946

Late one night a Partyman knocked at our door.
– How are you all? he asked.

We're gathering the household together, getting order once
    more,
Looking after each other. A good guest sees no wrong!

Out in the street the world was cold and white,

Out in the street was the wild blown snow and the night.
Our guest came in with a smile, like an old friend.
Out in the street the snowstorm keened and cried
And cast in a flurry on wall and gable-end
Its frozen lacy fragments like foam on the tide.
Our guest threw open his greatcoat and listened to the
    blizzard,
Our guest threw open his greatcoat and the medals glittered.
– Coarse weather this, just like the south! That moaning!
Do you know the great Black Sea storms?
                   – We've known them.
And so our talk moved on, to friends and wives,
To war and victory, to glad and grieving lives.
And now it seemed the whole house breathed and strained
Out like a ship that smells the open sea.
It seemed as if the walls rolled back and we
Saw the whole world by reef, harbour, and strand,
Saw our whole land lying by other lands,
So vast, and yet so young, who understands?
The silent fields hide their harvest and power.
Far off the lightning-flickers fade in flight.

Clock-chimes float down from the snowy tower.
The night is late. Moscow lies cold and bright.

There is something in the tone here, and in the engagement with human encounter in a fairly desolate urban scene, that recalls Morgan's 1960s Glasgow poems which made such an impact on his readers. 'Good Friday', 'In the Snack-bar' and 'Trio' (CP: 164, 170, 172) are still studied in the curriculum of Scottish schools.

Those poems were still, however, a decade in the future. In early 1956, the Cold War had seemed to be edging a degree or so closer to normality when, in February, the new Russian leader, Nikolai Kruschev, attacked Stalin's policies, and then later in July the Stalinist leader in Hungary, Mátyás Rákosi, was forced to resign. All further hopes were dashed by November, however, when Russian tanks imposed a brutal pacification on Budapest, with an estimated thirty thousand dead. But in 1955, Morgan's focus on Russian poetry may have been part of his longing for a more informed and peaceable understanding between West and East, with acts of translation as his contribution to a hoped-for 'thaw'.

His use of Scots language was a way of bringing such understanding closer to home. Mikhail Lermontov (1814–1841) was descended from a Scottish family, Learmonth (as was Morgan, coincidentally, on his mother's side). Lermontov is not clearly represented in *Collected Translations*, but a translation into Scots of Heine's 'Ein Fichtenbaum steht einsam' (CT: 404) is in fact a re-translation of Morgan's English version of a Russian version by Lermontov dated 1841 (UGL: MS Morgan E/1/2/1). The poem was done first in English in July 1955, but in January to February 1956, while he was doubtless also considering his Seminar presentation, Morgan revisited the Russian/German and found a more authentic Scottish voice for both poets:

In northern wilds, on a naked ridge
    There stands a lonely pine.
It sleeps as it sways, all swathed in snow,
    Stiff in a stole of rime.
And this is its dream: of far-off sands,
    Lands where the high sun glows
And alone and in chains on the burning rock
    The glorious palm-tree grows.

And in Scots:

Yonder's a lanely fir-tree
On the Hielan moors sae bare.
It sleeps in the snaw and the cranreuch
And a cauld plaid mun wear.

It dreams aboot a palm-tree
Murnan alane in the east –
Murnan for aye in the silence
On a desert's clinty breist.

'Cranreuch' is hoarfrost, 'mun' is must, and 'clinty' is stony. Beyond dictionary glosses stands the authenticity of proletarian speech. After the Union of Parliaments in 1707, the government of Scottish affairs went south, and there was a loss not only of parliamentarians and power to Westminster but of a current Scots language of governance. Gradually vernacular Scots became identified with domestic life, trade, agriculture and working-class oral discourse. But its continuing literary power to move listeners and readers was clear from the wide success of the poetry of Robert Burns later in the century. Morgan's political concerns for working-class poverty in industrial Glasgow made his choice of Scots language one of solidarity. He had already begun to try Mayakovsky in Scots, publishing 'Mayakonferensky's Anectidote' (CT: 129) in *Lines Review* 4, January 1954. It would not be surprising if this was the issue of the magazine that he had left with Ykaterina Shevelyova.

On his return from Russia he gained some experience of the realities of Soviet publishing and the reach of the state. His translations of Shevelyova's poem 'The Cranes' and of Mayakovsky's 'Anent the Deeference o Tastes' (CT: 151. 'Anent' means 'concerning') were printed in the *Soviet Weekly* of 13 October 1955. But the editors censored the few 'critical' observations Morgan had made in his accompanying account of the study tour. He had made the mistake of commenting on the somewhat confusing contrast between 'the drab outward appearance of things and the obvious happiness and animation of the people'. Of course, only the happiness and animation of the people survived in the published article.

I wonder now whether Mayakovsky made his way into the *Soviet Weekly* simply because the censors could not translate the Scots language of the translation. And yet Morgan never lost a sense of the 'animation and happiness of the people', and the possibility of moments of tenderness and enthusiasm in a workaday post-revolutionary world. This seemed to be carried particularly on the faces and voices of women. That was a new departure for him, and also a revolution in its way. Here are two uncollected portraits of women on the move, the first translated from Lina Kostenko and the second from German Florov. These would be published in *Soviet Literature* 12, in December 1957, under the heading, 'Englishman Translates Soviet Poetry':

IN THE ELECTRIC TRAIN

The birch-trees rush towards the train,
The day is breaking, the windows glow;
The girl with weariness in her face
Still leans against me as we go.
'Night-shift?' 'Yes, I – (here she gave
A vague glance round) '– so want to sleep...'
Then she curled up, dropped off, and made
A pillow of my shoulder. Keep
On sleeping, weary-head. I hate
to wake you, I hate to disturb you there.
Dear comrades!
                      Here's my stop. My place
You must take over: so quietly, and with such care!

THE WOMAN

She brought into the compartment with her
The spicy scent of Siberian pines.
The blizzard, as if tired of drifting,
sleeps in a downy shawl. Snow shines
Briefly where a flake is melting
On her lashes; she blinks, her eyes screwed up...
The Major smoothed his cigarette; his
Match remained in the air, unstruck.
The architect took off his glasses
With care from laughing hazel eyes.
Again as we listened we saw the fabulous
New Siberian township rise.
The train sped on.
                    The woman was gazing
At the slumberous volcanic hills.
She was silent; it was nothing she was singing or saying
That caught and fused their separate wills
To read her profile, her clear forehead;
They saw the far had come near, they could pass
Into the fabulous life of the forest.
Their tea reached them sweet in the glass.

Three Poems

JAMES LEO MCASKILL

The Norseman's First Summer

Fok-pykkr, in rás sæti
the leave-gone from water mountain

day, day, day, black-day, ne slæpe,
see dust yellow, push, push, live,

vision, ne boll, kið, geit, geit-punnr, live
tree small, mansize, unstrong

green maker yellow oil and hot, beard
and wine hot. Kið, geit, tree-small

unsnowed, unvile land, fok-punnr
wifmen-light, light wimmen, housers

uncolded, unfat, black, dark-soft
yellow-oil wifmen in this tree-small.

Fok leg-spread by skeið, vǫlvur
in song-lag, ear-turners dream

in day-passion, skeið to edgewater
to vǫlvur, fok-pykkr and slæpe.

Labour

They say it is the oldest profession.
Older than the sea-vacuuming fishermen;

the proverbial sheep-and-goatherds;
the sweat-faced smiths and smith's apprentice

unable to find a girlfriend on an unsalaried
internship, sharing a room south of the river;

the milliners; the winemakers; the builders,
dragging slop mud into squares of dry mudbrick

for a mosque and a house and a brothel;
the accountants; the taxmen; all those

of jobs immoral enough to bring about
religious conversion, a change of heart,

hold a burgeoning civilisation together;
the cross-makers; the athletes;

those who did things with wood
before the Romans; the transubstantiationists;

the producers of religions and religious stories;
the road-footed messengers;

the breakers of horses and donkeys;
the finders of navigable routes over mountains

through seas and forests and marshland;
the stalkers, approachers and fellers of deer

elephant, buffalo, whale and whale shark;
the singers; the incorrigible upright walkers.

Well, with all this work being done
why shouldn't a woman have a job?

Days

They are cleaning the bells in Viterbe.
The bus is near Urbino.

The oak-green cascades are falling in the North-West.
A sheep is watching the sea hit the rocks.

Rick is doing his loft in the sunset.
Brown clouds are above Nantong.

Justinian bathes, and drinks the water he bathes in.
A film projector loops *Gone with the Wind*.

Coventry is twinned with Dresden.
Sarcasm is invented, then contravened.

The fish eat at a shipwreck of fingers and gold.
A century turns to another.

Laura never looks the same in any two pictures.
Hiro and his wife are at a weighing.

The unpeopled earth is illuminated by a billion stars.
The toes are going through the grapes.

Nobody ever bothers to call.
The people in the rainforest have never heard of the Portuguese.

Usman is feeling tired but doesn't know why.
They make the area into a national park.

A child's clitoris is removed with a piece of glass.
Gin is invented.

In the basement there are things no one should see.
Something is shimmering on the water, in the air.

Charlemagne regrets his trip to Rome.
Natale can only see his kids at weekends.

Women and Men rebuild the cathedral at Chartres.
They go out on the water in the rain.

What his father tells him, he tells his son.
The plane crashes in Munich in the snow.

Her waist bends to the will of her clothing.
The wanderers arrive at Skelig Michael.

They wait and wait but he never comes.
People scatter determinedly around the continents.

Ira wakes from a confusing dream.
The ancestors line the longhouse and sing

sing
sing.

On the Watch

JOHN LUCAS

WE ALL THINK we know Auden's dictum that poetry makes nothing happen. But we mostly misquote him. Because Auden didn't say quite what he's usually praised – and occasionally criticised – for saying. The last word, 'happen', is not followed by a full-stop but by a colon, following which the poet goes on to say that poetry survives

In the valley of its saying where executives
Would never want to tamper; it flows south
From ranches of isolation and the busy griefs,
Raw towns that we believe and die in; it survives,
A way of happening, a mouth.

A moralised or fabled landscape? Perhaps the river runs through Auden's favoured limestone country of 'short distances and definite places', far from the reach of officialdom, and free to flow into and meander about everyday life? The trick of reversing epithets – towns are naturally busy, griefs are often raw – is one Auden used on other occasions at this period. ('And when he cried the little children died in the streets.') Or is this not so much trickery as tricksiness, a way of avoiding his own subject – the death of W. B. Yeats.

Because Yeats certainly thought his poetry had made things happen. 'And did that play of mine send out / Certain men the English shot?' True, many years later Paul Muldoon asked sardonically, 'Would certain men have stayed in bed / If Yeats has saved his pencil lead?' ('7, Middagh Street' in *Meeting the British*.) But the answer, whether Muldoon intended it or not, was almost certainly, yes. Which isn't to say that poetry *will* make things happen, but that some of it, on certain occasions, undoubtedly does so. Easter, 1916, was one such occasion. And Auden, writing in 1939, couldn't have been ignorant of how, in the 'low, dishonest decade', then coming to an end, bad things had happened to poets precisely because they were poets. He may not have been aware of Mandelstam's fate, but he must surely have known about Gumilyov, can hardly not have suspected that the harsh criticism of 'individualism' to which Mayakovsky was subjected contributed to his suicide in 1930, knew of Lorca's squalid murder, and would have heard through Oxford friends if by no other means of the public burning in Athens of Ritsos's *Epitaphios,* a long poem written after the massacre of tobacco-workers in Thessaloniki in 1936. The Greek dictator, Metaxas, modelled this ostentatious display of State control on the Nazi book burnings, about which Auden also knew. Everyone did. Executives might not want to raid the ranches of isolation but totalitarian regimes had no such qualms. And yet 'tamper' – 'to meddle or interfere, so as to harm' – is too weak a word to account for what Stalin, Hitler, and Franco licensed, even if 'executive' in its then-current dominant meaning of 'designating the branch of government that deals with putting into effect laws and judicial sentences', suggests officialdom's suppression of free speech, which is one way of trying to ensure that poetry does *not* happen.

By 1939 Auden was in New York, the raw city from where he writes 'September 1, 1939', and it is at least arguable that the slipperiness of the lines from his elegy on Yeats can also be detected in the later poem. As both title and the use of trimeters make evident, Auden's poem is self-consciously echoing in order, perhaps, to challenge 'Easter, 1916', because, unlike Dublin, New York is a place where nothing can happen.

Faces along the bar
Cling to their average day:
The lights must never go out,
The music must always play.

These faces are very different from the ones Yeats evokes at the beginning of 'Easter, 1916': 'I have met them at close of day / Coming with vivid faces / From counter or desk among grey / Eighteenth-century houses.' Such vividness rebukes the 'polite, meaningless words' Yeats exchanges with the men and women he encounters and about whom he plans to report 'a mocking tale or a gibe, / To please a companion / Around the fire at the club'.

Yeats's great poem acknowledges his own culpability in mis-reading both the times and those whom he believes, like him, 'but live where motley is worn'. He may have been appalled by the historic moment, its 'terrible beauty', but he took it as his self-appointed responsibility to keep a watch on the moment as it happened. Auden, too, with the close-set eyes of mother's boy, intended to keep watch. Hence, his scrutiny of those faces, presumably seen in the glass behind the bar, for whom 'the conventions conspire / To make this fort assume / The furniture of home'. The bar on 51st Street is safe from the intrusions of history, or thinks itself to be so.

But who can live for long
In an euphoric dream;
Out of the mirror they stare,
Imperialism's face
And the international wrong.

There is, though, something wrong about this. The face that stares back at Auden may be his own but the other drinkers can hardly be said to reflect and so reveal their acknowledgement of 'Imperialism's face / And the international wrong.' Europe's war wasn't America's, not in 1939, and when Roosevelt two years later managed to persuade a reluctant America to join the alliance against the Axis powers he had no need to play on guilt feelings. For Auden to try to impute to New Yorkers such feelings is very different from Yeats's complex response to the faces into whose eyes he looks. Auden's lines may not amount to bad faith but they undoubtedly feel a bit dodgy. *He* may be guilty but *they,* the people along the bar, don't feel themselves to be so.

*

It was Auden who, in *The Enchafed Flood,* suggested that the undifferentiated crowd so regularly invoked in Edward Lear's limericks – 'they' – are not dissimilar from the sailors in 'The Rime of the Ancient Mariner' who in behaving en masse exhibit the stock response that is so often seen as opposed to and by the individual, whether ancient mariner or old man with a beard; the agedness adds pathos, makes mariner or bearded outsider not merely apart from 'the crowd' but its lonely victim. It's a familiar enough trope of modernism: on the one had the suffering, sensitive outsider; on the other, the crowd, 'they'.

Not long before Auden wrote the two poems mentioned above, Robert Frost published *A Further Range* (1936), which includes 'Neither Far Out Nor in Deep'.

The people along the sand
All turn and look one way.
They turn their back on the land.
They look at the sea all day.

As long as it takes to pass
A ship keeps raising its hull;
The wetter ground like glass
Reflects a standing gull.

The land may vary more
But wherever the truth may be –
The water comes ashore,
And the people look at the sea.

They cannot look out far.
They cannot look in deep.
But when was that ever a bar
To any watch they keep?

They turn their back. The singular 'back' allows for the people's uniformity of response in turning on the land. (It's at least arguable that the plural 'backs' would have been grammatically necessary if the people had turned them *to* the land.)

In his sympathetic study of Frost, *The Work of Knowing,* Richard Poirier says that the people in the poem exhibit 'a conformity of dull staring', and that the landscape (*sic*) is 'impoverished. It gives no sense to life; it promises little in the future, and none at all to the imagination'. To be strictly accurate, it's the sea which, in Poirier's account, is impoverished. The land may be more interesting than the sea, may 'vary more', though the people are unwilling or unable to recognise this. In which case the person uttering the poem, the onlooker, is an outsider, apart from the crowd, but watching it, keeping watch, able to judge it from a standpoint of superiority, perhaps condescension. The person who sits in the bar on 51st Street tries to present himself as one of many. He keeps watch on behalf of all, though they all want to be Mr Average. The person who looks at the people along the strand has no such intention.

And yet to read the poem that way doesn't feel right. The people *may* be like those who sit beside Auden in the bar on 51st Street, clinging to their average day, but equally well, I suggest, their 'watch' could be a kind of stoical acceptance of their lot. Though they can look neither far out nor in deep, they stick to their self-appointed task of confronting the uncertain world of the sea, which, especially for New Englanders, is the place of savage strangeness, where, as a famous line has it, blue-lunged combers lumber to the kill.

This is, I know, to read into the poem what Frost doesn't actually say. The people who watch the sea can't see that far out. They can't see anything much. To repeat Poirier's words, they are stuck with a dull staring. Other commentators have gone still further. I remember in particular an essay which appeared years ago in the magazine *Agenda* where the poem was 'unmasked' as a right-wing satire on fellow-travellers of the 1930s, all of them staring not so much at as across the sea – presumably toward Russia – and, blinkered by ideology, choosing to turn against the variousness of their own land. Ignorant and obtuse, the people along the strand form a lumpen, virtually de-humanised mass.

Well, it's possible. But if we find ourselves persuaded by this reading, how shall we respond to the following words?

When we choose between land and sea, the human and the inhuman, the finite and the infinite, the sea *has* to be the infinite that floods in over us endlessly, the hypnotic monotony of the universe that is incommensurable with us – everything into which we look neither very far nor very deep, but look, look just the same. And yet Frost doesn't say so – it is the geometry of this very geometrical poem, its inescapable structure, that says so. There is the deepest tact and restraint in the symbolism. It is like Housman's 'Stars, I Have Seen Them Fall' [...] But Frost's poem is flatter, greyer, and at once tenderer and more terrible, without even the consolations of rhetoric and exaggeration – there is no 'primal fault' in Frost's poem, but only the faint Biblical memories of 'any watch they keep'. [...] It would be hard to find anything more unpleasant to say about people than that last stanza, but Frost doesn't say it unpleasantly – he says it with flat ease, takes everything with something harder than contempt, more passive than acceptance. And isn't there something heroic about the whole business, too – something touching about our absurdity? [...] The tone of the last lines – or, rather, their careful suspension between several tones [...] allows for this, too. This recognition of the essential limitations of man, without denial or protest or rhetoric or palliation, is very rare and very valuable, and rather usual in Frost's best poetry.

I have felt it necessary to quote at some length from Randall Jarrell's great essay about Frost, 'To the Laodiceans', because I can't otherwise convey Jarrell's scrupulous regard for what he convinces me the poem is doing, is about. Critical writing of this order is also 'very rare and very valuable, and rather usual' in Jarrell's work. In this reading, the speaker-onlooker is less divided from 'the people', is even, at least implicitly, identified with them. Such sympathy may be less than complete – it may call to mind the distinction made between Wordsworth's power to feel *for* but never *with* the objects of his contemplation – but if we accept its presence as an essential element among the 'several tones' which Jarrell notes, then it follows that 'Neither Far Out Nor In Deep' can't be read as satire or disenchanted report by a lofty commentator on the inability of 'the people' to be other than incurious, complacent, torpidly conformist. The voice that speaks the poem is more democratic, less assertively authoritative, let alone authoritarian.

*

In his famous essay of 1940, 'Inside the Whale', Orwell, on the attack against fellow-travellers, condemned the Auden of 'Spain' as one of those who are 'always somewhere else when the trigger is pulled'. Auden hadn't fought in the Spanish Civil War, so what right had he to comment on 'the necessary murder'? By the time the essay appeared, Auden was in America, a long way from the action, and in the process of retreat from his earlier, more evident radicalism. I don't know whether he felt wounded by Orwell's attack, or even whether he thought there was justification in his words, but 'September 1, 1939' (which may have been written before he could have had a chance to read Orwell's essay) is, among other things, a kind of *mea culpa* for the preacher's loose, immodest tone. This doesn't, though, prevent Auden from uttering a kind of preacher's prayer, even if 'All I have is a voice / To undo the folded lie'. As Stan Smith has remarked, 'If you want to undo something that is folded, a disembodied voice is the last thing you need. What you need are *hands*. But the characteristic definition of the bourgeois subject, in poetry as in democracy, is that of the freely self-articulating voice.' True, but Auden's voice is now blended with others, those whom he characterises as 'the Just', whose 'Ironic points of light / Flash out wherever [they] / Exchange their messages.'

May I, composed like them
Of Eros and of dust,
Beleaguered by the same
Negation and despair,
Show an affirming flame.

I would say that without a shadow of doubt Auden is here picking up the images and meaning of a passage in E. M. Forster's essay 'What I Believe'. The essay was first given as a radio talk in 1938, when it was called 'Two Cheers for democracy', and in the following year was published under its new title. The 'voice' with which Auden hopes to undo the folded lie is, like Forster's, ironic, unofficial, deliberately anti-authoritative. Those in power, Forster said in his essay, 'become crooked and sometimes dotty as well', and although Auden can't match Forster's wonderfully wry refusal of a public tone, the ambition of 'September 1, 1939' is pretty certainly to recognise and honour the worth of private faces – nicer and wiser than public faces. But, to repeat, the poem's 'I' as well as its 'eye', insisting as it does on projecting guilt onto others, overdoes the speaker's authority. This is not so much knowledge as knowingness.

*

In the years 1946–7, Yannis Ritsos produced a clutch of poems to which he gave the title *Parentheses*. By then Ritsos, like the poor, was enduring the suffering to which he was fairly accustomed. Persecuted by the Metaxas dictatorship before the war, he remained in Athens during the terrible years of the German Occupation of Greece, spending much of the time in bed with tuberculosis – an illness from which he suffered throughout his life; then, in January 1945, after the Nazi retreat, he joined the National Operation Forces (EAM) in Northern Greece, writing plays for the People's Theatre of Macedonia, before returning to Athens where he worked as a copy-editor while retaining his commitment to the Communist Party and writing, as always, at full tilt. During this period he produced, among much else, *Parentheses*, including the following poem, 'Miniature':

The woman stood up in front of the table. Her sad hands
begin to cut thin slices of lemon for tea
like yellow wheels for a very small carriage
made for a child's fairy tale. The young officer sitting opposite
is buried in the old armchair. He doesn't look at her.
He lights up his cigarette. His hand holding the match trembles,
throwing light on his tender chin and the teacup's handle.
    The clock
holds its heartbeat for a moment. Something has been
    postponed.
The moment is gone. It's too late now. Let's drink our tea.
Is it possible, then, for death to come in that kind of carriage?
To pass by and go away? And only this carriage to remain,
with its little yellow wheels of lemon
parked for so many years on a side street with unlit lamps,
and then a small song, a little mist, and then nothing.

In the Introduction to his excellent *Ritsos in Parentheses* (1979) Edmund Keeley, whose translation is here quoted, says that the best of the poems 'are far from simple, for all their apparent focus on relatively simple things,' and he singles out 'Miniature' as 'among the subtlest and finest of the many hundred shorter poems that Ritsos has written. The simple things in this poem are an unidentified woman, an unidentified officer, some thin slices of lemon, an old armchair, a match, a cigarette, a teacup. And the action is really an absence of action: a visit that could lead to a meeting of some kind, a coming together that does not finally take place.'

While all of this is true, it should be added that what gives the poem its authority is, paradoxically, the seeming absence of any authorial presence directing our point of view, telling us how to respond to the miniature scene we glimpse. The poem seems not to have designs on us at all. Instead, it objectively sets before us 'simple things'. This, though, needs to be qualified. We can't after all see the 'side street with unlit lamps / and then a small song, a little mist'. Nor can we do more than infer the aching sense of incompletion in the moment when the clock 'holds its heartbeat', which we can't hear, any more than we can see the woman's 'sad hands' make lemon slices like 'a very small carriage [...] a child's fairy tale'. But these elements belong with the speculative atmosphere the poem generates. We have to work out for ourselves the significance of what we see. Is this woman the young officer's would-be lover? Or is she perhaps his mother? Does the hand holding the match that lights up his tender chin and the teacup's handle – the details have a filmic clarity – tremble because he can't bring himself to speak of love or because he's about to leave for a war from which he may well return as a corpse, laid on a carriage, an open hearse, that in future years may itself end up abandoned, in a side street, an out-of-date item from a forgotten, defeated world?

Ritsos won't answer the questions the poem sets up. He can't, because this is history in the making, a moment, a miniature, even if it allows for the possibility of long perspectives. (The Greek for miniature, *micrographia*, suggests an act of drawing.) In short, this is a poem which makes a moment of history happen for its readers. And for this to be so depends on the tactical withdrawal of the poet from his poem. We, as much as the poet, have to be on our watch.

Poetry in Motion

MAITREYABANDHU

I'd like to think of something critical to say about *Paterson*, Jim Jarmusch's near-perfect film-poem about the workings of the imagination, but I can't think of anything worth mentioning. Set in Paterson, New Jersey, a man called Paterson – whose hero William Carlos Williams also lived in Paterson, where he wrote a poem called 'Paterson' – drives a bus with 'PATERSON' on its destination indicator. Paterson (Adam Driver) gets up, leaves his girlfriend (Golshifteh Farahani), takes his morning stroll to the depot, drives, listens to snatches of conversations, returns home, walks the dog (an English bulldog), goes to same neighbourhood bar, drinks a beer, then walks back home again.

That's about it. The film is at pains *not* to be dramatic. On one of his walks with the dog, Paterson is waylaid by roughnecks in an open-top car who tell him that his dog is in danger of being dogjacked (the dog version of hijacked). Nothing happens to the dog. Walking home from the depot, Paterson notices a young girl alone, waiting for her mother. She has a 'secret notebook' and writes poems. She reads him one. No one calls the police or the Safeguarding Officer. Paterson's girlfriend buys a guitar they can't afford. They don't end up at one another's throat.

The actual poetry in the film – the words of which appear across the screen as Paterson composes them while eating Cheerios, or leaning on the steering wheel, or just 'walking dully along' – are written by the 74-year-old Oklahoma-born poet Ron Pagett. The poems are good, but *Paterson* is not a film about 'genius in the making' or 'great poetry'. It's about our instinctive need to create and the state of mind from which creativity arises.

Like any successful poem, the film shows (rather than tells) Paterson's heightened awareness: the commonplace buses and breakfast bars, beers and Laundromats seem to contain a mysterious *more*, a significance that is 'felt not known', as Robert Frost put it. This *more* is not to do with plot or drama; it's intrinsic to conscious life, a quality of attention in which teenagers discussing anarchism or men boasting about their (non-existent) conquests, are experienced as meaningful – without being able to say what that meaningfulness *means*.

A primary quality of any successful poem is *unity*, a sense of everything in the poem – form, tone, syntax, word choice – participating in a larger whole. In a good poem random or even conflicting elements are unified by the poet's deeper (and therefore more unified) perception. *Paterson* is a wonderful instance of this. Everything seems to animate some deeper, underlying meaning. This is symbolised in the film by Jarmusch's use of circles. From the larger circle of the film's timeframe (Monday to Monday), to the buses daily circular route, the round cupcakes his girlfriend bakes, the watch-face on Paterson's wrist, the Cherrios he eats, down to the pattern of the tiny circles on their bedsheets, *Paterson*'s circles within circles express the film's poetic unity: each detail is held within a larger unity; the larger unity is expressed in every detail.

The sense of the poem being 'just one word', as Don Paterson put it, is served in the film by thematic and visual echoes, mirrorings and doubles that stand in for poetry's refrains, rhymes and half-rhymes: the triple-joke about a fireball, for instance; the recurring name 'Paterson'. Early in the film Paterson's girlfriend dreams that they have twins together. Thereafter twins keep mysteriously appearing in the film. There is something uncanny about twins; they transgress our everyday expectations of life. They take us, as any good poem should, a little beyond habitual consciousness.

The unification of a poem (or film in this case) has the effect of unifying *us*. This unified awareness – where thought, feeling, intuition, and body-sense run together as a single whole – leads us to a deeper sense of ourselves and the world. The hints of the uncanny, even of transcendence in *Paterson*, come to a head at the end of the film. 'Transcendence' seems too grandiose a word for such an everyday setting – though where else are we to find it, the film wants to say, but in the ordinary, in the commonplace? Paterson meets a Japanese poet (Masatoshi Nagase) who is reading a dual-language edition of Williams's *Paterson*. The poet exudes a kind of courteous exoticism, a sense of the mystical East. He is symbolic of unified and therefore heightened perception; the *more* the poet discovers in the everyday.

Two Poems

ROWLAND BAGNALL

In the Funhouse

In *Superman: the Movie* (1978), Superman turns back time
by flying backwards round the globe. We see a rockslide
happen in reverse as Lois Lane emerges from the sinkhole
she's been crushed to death in, meaning that she never died
at all. In the Funhouse, a mirror shows me stretched, my head
caved in, the sole survivor of some hilarious near-fatal collision.

Halfway down an artificial indoor beach (running along a back
wall painted with what looked suspiciously like the Normandy
landings: upturned bodies on the sand, bits of bodies in the sea,
the constant sound of waves and cartoon screaming and explosions
coming from a speaker hidden somewhere in the ceiling) I wondered
if my limbs had returned to normal. The floor began to move in

circles at different speeds. The walls pressed slowly in around me.
Next door, a neon light shone on a plastic Christopher Reeve.
I made my hand into a fist and thrust it out in front of me which
did nothing, which didn't surprise anyone in the room, which
was only me, which didn't surprise anyone in the room. Crawling
through a tunnel on my hands and knees, I imagined Superman

saving me in a succession of perilous displays: trapped in the back
of a mechanically compressing car on a junkyard conveyor belt;
falling head-first from the topmost floor of a collapsing holiday
resort in Spain; cocooned in ropes and laid out on a railway track
by thugs. As I emerged, I was suddenly reminded of a scene in
a film, though couldn't remember which scene, or which film.

Viewpoint

In *Rear Window* (1954), Alfred Hitchcock suddenly looks at us
through the glass frame of an apartment penthouse, somehow
somewhere other than behind the camera's lens – viewed from
the perspective of James Stewart's binoculars – all but invisible
to anyone who doesn't know it's him. *Always make the audience
suffer as much as possible*, I thought, rains beginning on the roof.

From up here I could see a skydiver looking backwards at a plane
as if it was falling away from him and not the other way around.
The air was the same temperature as I was, still breathable and
warm but lightly thickening with something else, like vapours
pouring slowly from a car's exhaust. Away to the right I swore
I could see the monstrously reclining figures of a sculpture park,

misshapen and decayed, the stones displaying marks left by
the hurricanes of several years ago. Around the moment of
deployment, the parachutist feels a brief instance of shock
between the pulling of the ripcord and successful opening
of the main canopy. Convinced the mechanism has finally
failed, he tries to recall a succession of emergency techniques

before – at last – the canvas swells, jerking freefall to violent
and relieving halt. Throughout the film, a pianist composes
a song called 'Lisa'. His voice is never heard, appearing only
in long shots through the window. He seems to live alone but
for the one-time presence of the filmmaker standing several
feet behind him, winding an old clock on the mantelpiece.

--- R E V I E W S ---

Physical Pursuit

Richard Holmes, *This Long Pursuit: Reflections of a Romantic Biographer* (Collins, 2016) £25; Paul Farley and Michael Symmons Roberts, *Deaths of the Poets* (Cape, 2017) £14.99

Reviewed by TONY ROBERTS

RICHARD HOLMES is one of our best biographers, always in hot pursuit of his subjects. Since his passionately vivid *Shelley: The Pursuit* (1974) he has constantly returned to that image. In *Footsteps: Adventures of a Romantic Biographer* (1985), he describes biography as 'a tracking of the physical trail of someone's path through the past, a following of footsteps'. In *Sidetracks: Explorations of a Romantic Biographer* (2000) it is 'a personal adventure of exploration'. In *This Long Pursuit* Holmes goes even further: 'I had come to believe that the serious biographer must *physically* pursue his subject through the past. Mere archives were not enough. He must go to all the places where the subject had ever lived or worked, or travelled or dreamed.'

Holmes, then, is nothing if not a romantic biographer of the Romantics. His motivation, as he eloquently explained of Shelley, is that the 'life seems more a haunting than a history'. In *Coleridge: Early Visions* (1989) he claimed his subject must invade the reader's imagination as it had his, or 'I have failed to do him justice'. Now, in *This Long Pursuit* – and on a lighter note – he yearns to dance around the dinner table with Madame de Staël.

This new book is substantially autobiographical, a reworking of lectures, articles and introductions, the third of the trilogy after *Footsteps* and *Sidetracks*. For Holmes the last leg is 'a sort of eulogy: a celebration of a form, an art, and a vocation'. A work of discovery and rediscovery, it is arranged in three sections: 'Confessions', 'Restorations' and 'Afterlives'. Characteristically, he is keen for us to glimpse the biographer's craft as he sees it. He reveals, for instance, his own method of transcribing his 'pursuit': research detail is to be written on one side of a notebook page and personal responses on the other – 'The cumulative experience of the research journey, of being in my subject's company over several years, thus became part of the whole biographical enterprise.' Hence the empathy, the passion, and the material for these 'reflections'.

The first essay, 'Travelling', recounts with a touch of humour Holmes's geographical quests for Shelley, Stevenson and particularly Coleridge. The next, 'Experimenting', reminds us that the age of the Romantic poets was equally a great age of scientific discovery and innovation. Holmes explored this in *The Age of Wonder* (2008) and here recounts being daunted by the prospect of introducing that book in a lecture to the Royal Society. In 'Teaching' Holmes focuses on his design of an MA course at East Anglia. Given the transient nature of biographical knowledge – how perspectives change with period and access to new materials – he saw, in comparative biography, a new discipline. 'Forgetting' deals with 'nominative aphasia' and 'associationism', and 'Ballooning' begins with Holmes's adventures in the sport, before recounting how Poe fictionalised Coleridge's.

As well as bringing science back into the Romantic equation, Holmes has also been alert to the contribution of women to the history of thought. He devotes part two of his new book, 'Restorations', to a handful of writers and scientists who deserve greater recognition: Margaret Cavendish ('Poet, polemicist, feminist, satirist, aristocrat, naturalist, stylist, eccentric and survivor'); the Enlightenment writer Zélide ('I find an hour or two of mathematics freshens my mind and lightens my heart.'); the brilliant and exhausting conversationalist and writer Madame de Staël; the once-celebrated 'educational writer and champion of women's rights' Mary Wollstonecraft; and Mary Somerville, author of the best-selling *On the Connexion of the Physical Sciences* (1834) an early work of popular science. Interesting as these narratives are, they are inevitably sketchy. With his more famous male Romantics, Holmes has the luxury of focusing on one theme, the life being already much travelled over. Here we must trust to the potential in his claim that 'biography as a form is destined continually to challenge conventions of silence and ignorance'.

In the final third of the book, Holmes returns to his intimacy with these Romantic poets: Keats, Shelley, Coleridge, Blake and, in addition, Regency portrait-painter Thomas Lawrence. As the section title 'Afterlives' suggests, he is concerned with reputations, with what Keats called the 'posthumous existence'. He is interested in the myths that have encrusted his subjects and the biographies which have rescued them.

In the last essay Holmes turns to William Blake. He describes how Blake was painstakingly, even heroically, rediscovered by the Victorian Alexander Gilchrist and his wife, Anne, and then how Blake has variously served succeeding generations (I, too, once witnessed Allen Ginsberg chanting 'Little Lamb' while accompanying himself on squeeze box in Manchester, an image hard to dislodge).

There is great similarity between Richard Holmes and Gilchrist. As the latter's widow observed: 'He desired always to treat his subject exhaustively: [...] as a biographer to stand hand in hand with him, seeing the same horizon, listening, pondering, absorbing.'

¶ Like Holmes, Paul Farley and Michael Symmons Roberts are travellers. The irony is that in *Deaths of the Poets* they are trapped in a bad idea. Through exhaustive journeys, these well-known 'moonlighting poets' address the usual suspects to explore a 'toxic myth' that began in England with Chatterton: that poetry demands the ultimate sacrifice, that genius often dies young and violently. This frankly fatuous premise is the occasion for the two poets to gallivant around Europe and America as dark tourists, standing where Berryman 'landed', where O'Hara was swiped by the beach buggy, at the hedge hollow which was Keith Douglas's temporary grave. Of course in doing so they contribute to the very myth they are questioning. But to put their mission in their own words: 'This book is constructed from a series of pilgrimages to the death-places of poets we admire and love, poets whose deaths seem – one way or the other – to shed light on the image of the doomed poet, or to test its mythology.' On the next page they widen their remit: 'this is also a book about places and the charge we feel (or don't) from their associations with a writer'. This corollary is vital to the book's inclusiveness because many of their poets did not, in fact, die young or badly. Think Eliot, Moore, Stevens, Williams, Frost, Auden, R.S. Thomas.

Deaths of the Poets has an impressive living cast, also. Tours are conducted by poets Jo Shapcott and Sean O'Brien, Ian Duhig and Neil Astley, among others. The authors explore academic and scientific journals, quote Donald Davie, Helen Vendler, Billy Collins *and* Richard Holmes. They are well researched, insightful, highly informative and clearly passionate about the poetry. They also offer knockabout humour, wit and endearing obsessiveness: 'did Larkin leave the copier lid up and press the poem to the glass, and, if so, is there a black edging to the copy he made containing an image of the poet's hand or shirt-sleeve or wristwatch, preserved in fading toner?'

And yet... almost halfway into the book they pose the question: 'Are we better off without the lives (and especially the deaths) of poets intruding on their work?' Obviously they have decided not, and yet they repeatedly strike an apologetic note: 'As we head up Eighth Avenue, stopping to apply Factor 40 to our noses and earlobes because the sun has come out [...] we reflect on how a more rigorous approach to literary pilgrimage has been brought to bear on the subject, by people equipped with the necessary analytical tools.' As they are sorting through Thom Gunn's effects they 'begin to feel uncomfortable: nosy, grubby' and leave him in peace. They admit to feeling 'a bit squeamish' studying Larkin's all-but-destroyed diaries (though at least they decline to try on his glasses). Trespassing in Mametz Wood, on the trail of David Jones, they 'have a sudden conviction that we shouldn't be here'. This makes the reader uneasy.

They are outside Plath's flat on Fitzroy Road: 'For the first time on our travels, we're feeling like proper thanatourists, ghouls out to doorstep the living and chill them with news of their domestic ghosts.'

There is a Halloween note struck more than once, 'Did Louis [MacNeice] simply die of cold or was there something down in the dark that took to him?' In the vicinity of Anne Sexton's garage suicide, the poets are equally mysterious: 'Now we are here, it reveals itself to be an unstable place where the membrane that separates life from death is disturbingly thin.' At John Riley's murder site 'the area emits a grim force field'.

At the end the writers tell us they have 'been wary of turning this book into a necropolis' and they have largely avoided that. Yet perhaps that is what they should have done instead: begun their stories from the gravestones and not from the warm corpses.

Fireflies & Field

Terence Cave
Thinking with Literature: Towards a Cognitive Criticism
(Oxford University Press, 2016) £25

Reviewed by NICOLAS TREDELL

TERENCE CAVE AFFIRMS that 'literature itself provides the primary energies' of his latest book, but he draws on the volatile fuel of cognitive science to try to boost our understanding of what literature is and how it works – and to deepen our appreciation of literary texts. Literature, he contends, 'offers a virtually limitless archive of the ways in which human beings think, how they imagine themselves and their world' and this is, so to speak, a vast mobile library, whose documents 'thrive on mutation'. In 'the broad sense', literature is 'the most revealing *product* and *symptom* of human cognition, an outgrowth of one of the most fundamental of human cognitive instruments': language.

These are large but heartening claims after the dismal decades of the later twentieth century when literature, even or especially among some of those paid to teach it, was dismissed as an ideological illusion, while, paradoxically, the simultaneous burgeoning of creative writing courses suggested that there were a growing number of people eager to produce (something like) literature (even if their reading of it was sometimes sketchy). In affirming the value of literature, however, Cave also upholds a key tenet of cognitive criticism: that the processes by which we understand literature are continuous with the everyday processes by which we understand language and living.

Cave is well aware that linking the justification and interpretation of literature with cognitive science runs several risks – of misunderstanding and misappropriating scientific terms and concepts; of taking as gospel disputed or discarded scientific ideas; of a two-way reductiveness that can diminish both literature and science. But he thinks the enterprise worth undertaking and he outlines two main, interrelated criteria for what it should entail 'within literary studies as an autonomous discipline': 'a cognitive approach' should be able to provide 'both a general explanatory framework for the phenomenon we call "literature" and a set of tools for close reading of individual texts'.

The individual texts Cave reads closely and insightfully in this book range in size from the minuscule to the massy: they include Yeats's four-line poem 'The Balloon of the Mind' and Carl Sandburg's six-line poem 'Fog'; three lines from John Ashbery's poem 'A Call for Papers'; the opening line of Paul Éluard's 'La terre est bleue...'; the 'Dover Cliff' scene from *King Lear*; Jonathan Franzen's novel *The Corrections*; Conrad's *Lord Jim*; and (of course) Winnie-the-Pooh. In his readings, Cave draws on and develops several key ideas of cognitive criticism. One is 'underspecification', the absence of specific information that might pin down a text's meaning more precisely, which means that the reader, to comprehend the poem, must perform further interpretative work (of a pleasurable rather than onerous kind). Underspecification, while especially salient in a short poem like 'The Balloon of the Mind', or in a haiku or epigram, is, Cave contends, a virtually 'universal condition of all language use'; we can never 'spell everything out' in words, so everyday communication, like literature, relies a great deal on 'implicatures', a term Cave takes from relevance theory to denote the intended meanings inferable from a particular utterance (as distinct from 'implications', which include unintended meanings).

Cave emphasises how 'The Balloon of the Mind', which starts with the word 'Hands', has 'a haptic character': 'the feel of the balloon, the pull on the ropes, the sheer implied awkwardness or friction of the encounter'. From this, he develops a more general point about 'kinesis' – that is, 'the transmission [...] of motor activation which the observer of some salient action or physical sensation feels as a neural readiness to perform the same action'. Such readiness can be triggered by observing someone in the flesh but also by language in its everyday and literary uses: it is a 'ghost' feeling which, while 'usually fleeting', results from 'activity in the neuronal area associated with the action in question'.

'Kinesis' is linked with 'mind-reading'; the latter process does not involve telepathy but the attribution of 'particular intentional states' to another person by inferences from their written, spoken and (if visible) body language. In this sense, human beings read minds all the time (not, of course, always accurately) in trying to communicate with one another and they also read minds when they read literature, attributing intentional states to narrators, dramatised speakers and characters. In the court scene in *Lord Jim*, for example, Conrad/Marlow evokes Jim's physical and mental feelings in a way that enables the reader to enter 'the domain of fully kinesic mind-reading, where motor resonance, affective empathy, and more reflective modes of inference operate seamlessly together to render a living model of the other's "subjective" experience – what it felt like at that moment to be Jim'.

A further key concept Cave deploys is 'affordance'. The American psychologist James J. Gibson coined this term to indicate 'what the environment offers the animal, what it provides or furnishes, either for good or ill'. A tree, for example, affords a bird a place to rest or nest. Human beings have vastly extended their range of artificial affordances but may still get out of kilter with them. Cave quotes the scene in *The Corrections* in which Chip's father Alfred, assailed by Parkinson's and related ailments, tries and fails to sit down on a chaise longue, an affordance that no longer affords a seat because of the neurological and motor impairment of a would-be sitter. Cave asserts that language 'is for humans the key empowering affordance' and that the 'successful affordances are the ones that enable us to grasp multiple phenomena as packages, or as integrated wholes' without eliding or diminishing 'the seething mass of particular things that inhabit them'. In Cave's erudite, elegant and entertaining book, literature clearly affords a stellar example of a successful affordance, its 'tiny points of living light' enabling, conditionally, large inferences: a process epitomised in the quote, which appears on the back cover and as an epigraph, from the late poet and astrophysicist Rebecca Elson (1960–99): 'As if, from fireflies, one could infer the field ...'.

On the Side of the Highway

Reginald Gibbons, *How Poems Think* (University of Chicago Press, 2015) $25

Reviewed by EVAN JONES

REGINALD GIBBONS BEGINS this study with the qualification that his reading of poems is somewhere between Donald Davie's 'resolve not to write in a way that is not a challenge to himself as he is' and Helene Cixous's 'unforeseen, unanticipated, and even apparently mistaken articulation [which] is the invaluable entrance to imaginative freedom'. One very English, the other very French, *naturellement*. But it's quickly apparent that Davie will take centre stage, and that he'll be overacting. There is a strange sort of combativeness to Gibbons's reading of Davie, which may well have to do with this quote, garishly flashing like hazard lights on the side of the highway in chapter 1:

By the time I last talked with him, on the occasion of a celebration of his career at Vanderbilt University in 1988, the year of his retirement and, at last, return to England, we had not seen each other for years, and in a letter he had sent me in 1986, he had expressed his hope that I would never again write poems like those in my book of that year.

Ah yes, here's a carwreck. The first chapter is all like

this, more the beginnings of a biographical piece on Davie and the sixties than criticism as such – and like nothing else in the book. I can't tell if this is axe-grinding or not on Gibbons's part, because he acknowledges Davie's importance clearly. And yet. What he does in chapter 1 draws out something of Davie's character. But at the same time, Gibbons doesn't take Cixous to task in such a way – even as he admits a personal connection to her. With Davie, something else is at stake, something unexpressed.

From there, the book develops more like a collection of essays than a coherent, developed study. There are important considerations of rhyme in Russian poetry, discussions of classical Greek poetry, and there are brilliant moments of incisive commentary. Gibbons is fascinating in his reading of classicist Gregory Nagy's interpretations of Pindar against nineteenth-century French literary critic Charles Augustin Saint-Beuve. What's central are the important differences between our poetry and that of the Ancient Greeks, where most tend to focus on the similarities. Particular emphasis is on the reader's role in the poem, which is insightful and intriguing, and suggests some of the ways in which our current ideas of poetry come together in Saint-Beuve's notion that 'one wishes poetry to be almost as much in the reader as in the author'. That wish might go some way towards explaining why the largest demographic of poetry readers is poets.

But one of the major problems with Gibbons's thinking is set out in the introduction, and there is never a satisfactory resolution: 'I have read through the *Oxford Book of English Verse* looking for examples of rhyme that leads the poetic thinking rather than solely ornamenting the poem, and there is very little...' Elsewhere in his readings of poems, Gibbons points out the importance of consonance, alliteration and even internal rhyme to meaning, but somehow endrhyme is just sittin' pretty. It's frustrating, because

it may well be that Gibbons sees only ornament in the rhymes of Wyatt or Shakespeare or Marvell or Bradstreet or Dickinson, but there is always meaning. Poets write into rhyme. When Wyatt rhymes 'hind', behind,' 'mind', and 'wind', readers can put together quickly what he's getting at. Rhyme is part of the evidence of what is happening: the hind, and its 'behind' no doubt, are all in the poet's 'mind', which is to say an erotic fantasy, followed by the invisible wind. Evidence. Every undergraduate student knows on first reading that something isn't straightforward in George Herbert's clanging, 'You must sit down, says Love, and taste my meat: / So I did sit and eat.'

An English-language poem, as Justin Quinn has written, can be read from right to left. This is another way in which it differs from prose and is one of the most important facets of its process of thinking. Endwords, rhyming or not, have weight, even when they don't appear to. Think of all those lines of Frank O'Hara's ending with 'I' as a reaction against the weightiness, a satire of it. Or look more closely at the Hudibrastic rhyme of Seidel and Muldoon (neither cited in Gibbons's book), and their influence on a younger generation, now active and well-received: Michael Robbins, Anthony Madrid and, closer to home, Adam Crothers. Muldoon, in his infamous sonnet 'Quoof', reveals what the poem is really about by purposefully not rhyming 'English' and 'language' in the sestet. Madrid *is* cited in a later chapter for his references to ancient civilisations, but not for his formal achievements. Instead, as a closer, there is a section of William Carlos Williams's *Spring and All*, which Gibbons uses as an example of the book's ideas at work. This is fine, but it is only one kind of poem.

The thinking about poems in *How Poems Think* is constructed with much understanding and care, based on a life reading, researching and teaching. And yet within all of that, it feels like a book with very clear limits: *How some poems think* is a more telling title.

Making Amends

Donald J. Childs, *The Birth of New Criticism. Conflict and Conciliation in the Early Work of William Empson, I. A. Richards, Laura Riding, and Robert Graves* (Montreal & Kingston: McGill-Queen's University Press, 2014) $110 CAD

Reviewed by MARK THOMPSON

HERE IS A STORY about the afterlife of New Criticism. As a student in Sarajevo in the mid-1980s, the Bosnian writer Aleksandar Hemon (b. 1964) came under the sway of a professor who 'taught a course in poetry and criticism'. This was Nikola Koljević, and 'Cleanth Brooks was his patron saint'; his first book was called *The Theoretical Foundations of New Criticism*. A few years after Hemon graduated, Koljević became one of the Serb leaders in the war against Bosnia. Fluent in English, tweedy in

appearance, he was much deployed with foreign journalists, mocking the accusations against his own side. His signature is on the treaty that ended the war in 1995. Two years later he killed himself.

In Koljević's class, Hemon 'learned how to analyse the inherent properties of a piece of literature, disregarding politics, biography, or anything external to the text. [...] we unpacked poems like Christmas presents'. During the war, he became obsessed with his old professor. 'I'd been mired in close reading, impressionable and unaware that my favourite teacher was involved in plotting a vast crime.' He was determined to 'unlearn' the approach to literature that Koljević had taught. 'I excised and exterminated that precious, youthful part of me that had believed you could retreat from history and hide from evil in the comforts of art.'

'Racked with guilt', the victim blamed – whom else – himself. Victim of what? The illusion that literature can be understood with formal tools that analyse its coherence, unity and self-completeness in terms of irony, paradox, ambiguity and so forth. That Koljević had been plotting years before seems unlikely; his entry into politics took people by surprise. It probably surprised him, too. Any deception practised on his students had worked first on himself. Immersion in New Criticism fostered, I dare say, a moral dulling or blindness, nudging intellectual principle and social ethics farther apart. Hemon's disabuse was cruel, though not different in kind from the awakening to the truth about fiction that comes with growing up.

Reading Donald Child's book, pause is first given by the sheer assumption of continuity between his title and subtitle. Of these figures, only Richards resembles a New Critic, and the likeness is skin-deep. The canard that Empson was a New Critic before the fact was exposed so long ago that one wonders how Childs took it seriously. In my case, the teacher (J. B. Steane) who read to sixth-formers from *The Well Wrought Urn* also read something from *Seven Types of Ambiguity*. Cleanth Brooks offered a kit for interpretation that felt antiseptic yet comforting because a bit of intellectual control goes a long way at eighteen. William Empson's swashbuckling engagement with poetry, life and the world, on the other hand, enthrals unforgettably when you are learning about all three as best you can.

It turns out that Childs's judgement has been clouded by suspicion. Not many histories of literary criticism are driven by a will to make amends; this is one. He argues that the true begetter of close reading was Robert Graves, latterly with Laura Riding in their book *A Survey of Modernist Poetry* (1927). Their roles have been insufficiently recognised 'in the prevailing narrative of the origins of New Criticism'; the parts played by I. A. Richards and Empson have been overestimated; and Empson churlishly withheld credit, especially from Riding.

Childs's outline case is fair: 'The principles [Empson] discovered in the work of Riding and Graves constituted both a motivating force for beginning his book and an informing presence throughout it.' Further allegations are sour: 'very much of what [Empson] has to say' about language, writing and reading was 'copied out of Riding and Graves'. The examples cited do not support this. Asked in later life why he had not acknowledged Riding in *Seven Types*, except for an errata slip inserted in the first edition following her and Graves's protest, Empson professed to have believed that his debt was to Graves, who was credited in later editions. This was shifty; *A Survey of Modernist Poetry* was explicitly collaborative, and Empson should have respected this, whatever his opinion about the likely authorship of those parts of the book that mattered most to him.

Whether Graves really was responsible for the crucial analysis of Shakespeare's Sonnet 129 remains contested. Childs strongly denies it, but without much argument. The same denial has been issued by Mark Jacobs ('Contemporary Misogyny: Laura Riding, William Empson and the Critics – a Survey of Mis-History', *English*, 246 (2015), pp. 222–240), again without solid evidence. Jacobs sees Empson as dependent on Riding's method of analysing Sonnet 129, but also as having misunderstood and misapplied that method ('every page of *Seven Types of Ambiguity* tackles the nature of 'ambiguity' along the lines he mistakenly took as laid down in *A Survey*'). Does this not suggest that Empson was inspired to depart from her method (described by Jacobs as being based on 'a principle of examining each and every word', which was hardly Empson's way) rather than stealing and misapplying it? Or even that Graves may have had more influence on Empson after all? Neither Childs nor Jacobs explains why they ignore Graves's later corroboration of Empson's hunch: 'I was, I believe, responsible for [...] showing the complex implications of Sonnet 129'.

This is not to excuse Empson's slighting of Riding's role in *A Survey*, rudeness that Jacobs charges to 'common-or-garden misogyny'. Certainly it seems more than an oversight. And Childs is correct that Riding's influence on Empson 'remains unresolved'. I think Empson found two separate but linked things in Graves and Riding: there was a theory about psychological conflict and poetry, which came from Graves, who had evolved it from W. H. R. Rivers; and there was a method of verbal analysis, which came from Riding and Graves combined. In his valuable book *Ambiguities*, reviewed in *PNR* 212, D. S. Reid argues that Empson's 'attachment to conflict theory was persistent. It is the solid thing behind his asserting that Graves, and not Riding, influenced him.' (p. 146) This puts Empson's rudeness in the best available light; the two separate things were linked in his mind, with the former eclipsing the latter. Corresponding with Riding in 1970, Empson said that 'the Conflict Theory of Poetry' was the 'necessary background for a theory of poetical ambiguity'. No doubt, but this does not mean Graves must have originated 'the method of analysis' that Empson adapted in *Seven Types*. What's needed still – surprisingly, given all this attention – is a meticulous comparison of Riding's and Graves's approach in *A Survey* with Empson's in *Seven Types*.

With three hundred pages still to go, one already feels that nothing would satisfy Childs short of Empson's signed confession. Fortunately, his account of these relationships, albeit grinding and repetitious, has real value. He is best when summarising and analysing Graves's four short critical books published between 1922 and 1926, which set out many of the ideas that were developed in *A Survey of Modernist Poetry* (1927), the historic collaboration with Riding. Like much interwar writing in the human and social sciences, these books breathe a larger air. They are energetic, witty, sweeping and provisional, blazing along a dozen avenues to an insight or axiom. Graves is thinking about what poetry is capable of, and fit for, in the post-war world. He is still recovering from shellshock, coming to terms with the experience of the trenches; and he wants poetry to figure and symbolically resolve the conflicts in his consciousness.

Childs's discussion of the 'conflict theory of poetry' is a model. *On English Poetry* (1922) has a chapter titled 'Conflict of Emotion' in which Graves claims 'emotional conflict is necessary for the birth of true poetry', indeed it is 'the whole cause and meaning of poetry'. Empson admitted much later to an (always) aggrieved Riding that the verbal analyses in this chapter had 'greatly struck' him because they proposed a 'healing process through the confrontation of opposed impulses'. This was, Empson added, 'the necessary background for a theory of poetical ambiguity, which he was approaching'. In *Poetic Unreason* (1925), Graves drew closer to this theory: 'Poetry may take the form of merely stating the nature of the conflict [or] the completer form of prescribing the cure of the ailment, suggesting how a new common life can be formed between these conflicting interests.' This sounds more like Richards than like Empson, yet Childs is right that a 'direct or indirect conversation with Graves about conflict can be found virtually everywhere' in *Seven Types*.

Even if Graves's thinking about conflict and conciliation were the source of New Criticism, the 'birth' took place not in the 1920s but a decade earlier, on the Western Front and then at Craiglockhart hospital, where his friend and fellow officer Siegfried Sassoon was treated by W. H. R. Rivers, whom they both came to venerate. The original conflict in 'the "conflict" theory of poetry' was the First World War. Graves's ideas were shaped by Rivers, the dedicatee of *On English Poetry*, who provided theoretical links from dream to poetry. Graves supported the practical psychotherapeutic mission of Rivers, who wanted his patients to recover. In Childs's telling, Empson found his place midway between Graves on one hand, who welcomed Freudian ideas (adapted by Rivers) and was happy to speak of 'different selves within the individual', and Richards on the other, who abjured these ideas until the mid-1930s. Empson once conceded that some modern poetry was 'carried through almost as a clinical thing', which is a nod to therapy. More usually his equivalent of 'cure for ailment' was his concern with the process of making decisions.

As well as showing Empson how to scan syntactical ambiguity, Graves and Riding defined interpretive principles that marked him for life. Childs quotes the heady remarks that follow their analysis of Sonnet 129:

Shakespeare's punctuation allows the variety of meanings he actually intends; if we must choose any one meaning, then we owe it to Shakespeare to choose at least one he intended and one embracing as many meanings as possible, that is, the most difficult meaning.

This is why the 'most final' meaning 'is always the most difficult'. As Shakespeare did not state his intended meaning in other words, we can only infer it (if we think it matters). Among the grounds for selecting among inferences, Graves and Riding choose inclusivity, encompassing as much meaning as possible. This is 'owed' to the author because there is a duty to let the poem be as good as it can be. This is the application to poets and poems of liberal policy to encourage individual human flourishing. As intention is finally unknowable, any other approach risks denying a poem its best meaning and hence its true value. Within the scope of intention, which may be partly unconscious, quality correlates with quantity; this is the basis of Richards's economy of impulses and Empson's rather simpler utilitarianism. (None of this would, I suppose, have meant much to Nikola Koljević.)

Turning to I.A. Richards, Childs builds another exhaustive case that Graves went 'unrecognised and unacknowledged'. This is more interesting because Richards and Graves had much in common; they attributed salvific power to poetry, attaching huge importance to its potential for psychological conciliation and for strengthening citizenship (by increasing people's interpretive competence). Their terminology was also close; they shared what Childs calls a faith in the 'psychological mechanism' that 'poetry stimulates in the reader the reconciliation of contradictory, or opposed, or divergent impulses'.

Why then did Richards single out Graves for censure in *The Principles of Literary Criticism* (1924), citing his analysis of 'Kubla Khan' as a portent of what a 'thoroughgoing Freudian onslaught' could do to literary understanding? Childs cannot account for it; I suppose they had enough in common for differences to grate, and their styles as writers were far apart. (Curious, by the way, for a non-combatant to use the metaphor of onslaught against a veteran recovering from shellshock. As it was curious to write a few years later, in *Practical Criticism*, of 'the atrocities which teachers sometimes permit themselves' when 'making a paraphrase or gloss'.) Accepting that Coleridge's unconscious was at work, Richards ruled that it drew not on private conflicts but on reading (*Paradise Lost*, Book IV). How odd that Richards could believe he had rebuffed Graves instead of deepening his interpretation.

There is always more than enough ingratitude to go around. Allegations have a way of multiplying. Childs believes Graves too is guilty, for he 'lifts quite a bit of material' from Frederick C. Prescott's *The Poetic Mind* (1922). It is dispiriting to think like this about influence, let alone inspiration. We should see it as the price of useful thoroughness. His sequel might examine a graver miscarriage: how the liberating enquiries of modernist criticism were captured, tamed and Taylorised by American universities, then exported as far as Sarajevo and beyond.

Tell Me More

William Wootten, *The Alvarez Generation: Thom Gunn, Geoffrey Hill, Ted Hughes, Sylvia Plath and Peter Porter* (Liverpool University Press, 2015) £25; *Clasp: Late Modernist Poetry in London in the 1970s,* ed. Robert Hampson & Ken Edwards (Shearsman, 2016) £12.95; Andrew Duncan, *A Poetry Boom 1990–2010* (Shearsman, 2015) £14.95

Reviewed by MICHAEL DANIELS

WHEN POETRY WAS characterised by dominant movements and critics were truly opinion-forming, Penguin's 1962 anthology *The New Poetry*, with Al Alvarez's introductory essay 'Beyond the Gentility Principle', crystallised a manifesto, or at least a taste, which helped define the poetic agenda for a generation. This essay, a 'contemporary pulse-taking', now serves as 'a significant record of the mood and obsessions of the time', and the starting point for Wootten's impressive reassessment.

'Obsessions' is apposite, and hovering behind the book is the question of how far Alvarez was simply reflecting what he observed, and how far he shaped public reception with his ideas of what poetry ought to be, and his appropriation of poets who became known as The Group.

Wootten traces Alvarez's debt to the critical ideas of Leavis, Empson and others, and much of the argument circles around an Aristotelean idea of the relationship between sincerity, seriousness and truth. Alvarez conceived of a poetry, in contrast to the 'good taste, clear syntax' and 'even tone' of The Movement, which could accommodate Modernism in the form of Eliot's technical and formal intelligence, alongside a Lawrentian willingness to peer unflinchingly at the pain and violence of the psyche, 'nakedly, and without evasion'. Poetry made in this way would embody the Leavisite imperative to transcend its own artifice and speak to life directly.

The conflation of psychic pain with strong poetry was central to Alvarez's conception, and the first edition of *The New Poetry* produced distinct models in the urban-sexual aggression of Thom Gunn's early poems, and (ignoring his transpersonal interests), Hughes's nature-violence axis as symbol of individual psyche. But it is in the account of Alvarez's relationship to and influence upon Sylvia Plath's work that this conjunction is most convincingly explored, particularly in Wootten's discussion of *The Savage God*. The surely exhausted archetype of the tortured artist threatens to engulf here, and Alvarez certainly made comments which might excuse the indulgence, (not helped perhaps by his adoption of the label 'extremist' poetry later in the sixties), but Wootten steers a calm and tactful course. Consequently his account of Plath's use of self-dramatisation as much as frank confession (both expressions of a 'performed self' and both 'routes out of Robert Lowell') is subtle and convincing, and helps orientate us to later critical responses. The impulse to self-dramatise is generally framed in pejorative terms in the case of Plath, yet, as Wootten establishes in his discussion of Veronica Forest-Thomson's critique, postmodern anxieties about the instability of words suggest Plath's strategies of dramatisation and projected personae may have been one of her most significant resources.

Wootten frames all this within influential psychological ideas of the time, particularly Ronnie Laing's extended excursions into anti-psychiatry, and notions of divided and authentic (integrated) psyches, which found their way into Alavrez's thinking and later contributed to a charge of neo-romanticism. The nub of this, in Freudian terms, is that he increasingly undersold the socialising and limiting force of the superego (for which, in poetic terms, we might read formal intelligence), so taken was he with the unbounded and unmediated expressions of the id, with Mailer's 'rebellious imperatives of the self'.

Wootten also teases out the possibilities Alvarez perceived in confessional and self-dramatising registers to sustain a tension between individual psychic pain and the atrocities of History. His account of this identification in terms of Alvarez's and Plath's Jewish and German heritages respectively, enacted in the context of the Eichmann trial and Cold War escalations, adds to the compelling scholarship.

To consider the force of Alvarez's argument, ultimately, is to consider the force of his prose, which is considerable, and in part explains why his contribution continues to fascinate; yet the idea that uncompromising self-examination might equate to a form of poetic truth seems too easy, and Wootten grounds his account in close critical reading rather than obvious answers. Peter Porter, who emerges as a more ambivalent figure in the Alvarez circle, questioned the 'poetics of authenticity': 'I have written a dozen books / to prove nothing can be done in words.' Gunn later rejected Alvarez's conception of sincerity, arguing for one closer to Hardy's and the speech of a 'sample human being'. Alvarez later acknowledged as much, regretting perhaps the extent to which 'we turned rashness and despair into literary principle'. This is particularly moving in the light of Alvarez's own struggles with depression and suicidal ideation at the time, the treatment of which, alongside the other suicides here, serves to humanise the debate beyond a straightforward literary scuffle. And as 'the serious gives way to ludic scepticism' in more and more contemporary poetry, it is good to be reminded of a time when much more seemed at stake.

¶ *Clasp* is an exercise in collective remembering, from a place and time when immersed poetic engagement outweighed any thought of creating a permanent record. Some putative contributors, we learn, couldn't remember, others didn't want to, and there is a tension between the impulse simply to record everything before it is too late, and a desire to reanimate events in high-resolution detail.

The seventies was, it turns out, a striking decade, sandwiched between counter cultural and Thatcherite revolutions, and the nature of experimentation was 'rhizomatic' between both practitioners and art forms. The small press explosion was axiomatic; readings and happenings abound; there were 'ranters and levellers, schisms and splits, and Earl's Court poetry wars', (Peter Barry's account in *Poetry Wars* is perhaps taken as read here) – a fierce sense of territory to be staked out through 'confusion, mess, vanity, incompetence [...] risk, excitement [...] some genius [...] brilliance'. The venues were rooms above pubs, municipal buildings – all, as it were, in public view, and more specifically not within the academy. The ensuing poetics of 'discontinuity and indeterminacy' went hand in hand with a broad politics of the liberal left. The Poets Conference, an embryonic trade union, argued for a minimum wage for poetry readings, alongside other brilliantly unquantifiable aims such as 'more poetry for more people', and small presses were ideological as well as practical (controlling the means of production). There were even claims of the CIA attending readings at the White House (!) pub to better understand the threat of guerrilla publishing, although ironically, small audiences were often a blessing since greater numbers reduced the chances of renewed Arts Council funding.

Initiatives such as the Modern British Poetry Conference, the Writer's Forum and Sub-Voicive fostered experiment within late Modernist templates, forming loose networks with other centres of activity in the British Poetry Revival. Others looked beyond Britain for a model, to the competing Modernisms of the New York and Black Mountain poets, for instance, or embraced 'the liberation of translation'. Key players emerge in all this: Eric Mottram, Bob Cobbing, Bill Griffiths, Ken Edwards, and significant poets and writers such as Allen Fisher, Tom Raworth and Iain Sinclair, although beyond these apparently more central male figures some of the more interesting accounts touch on the attempts of poets such as Frances Presley to combine Feminist ideas and agendas with linguistically innovative poetries.

There is much on affiliations and settings, but relatively little on actual working practices, which is disappointing for such process-driven work. Tantalising hints include 'people like Sylvia Hallett (with her bow and bicycle wheel)' – tell me more! – buildings as collaborators (the London Musicians Collective met in a disused British Rail laundry – 'you could flood it, light a fire in it, bounce rocks off it...'), work pioneering the medium of explosives – tell me much more! – and ultimately, for the general reader, it is these flashes of colour which provide the most fun.

¶ Offsetting reader expectation from the outset, Robert Duncan dismisses the idea of a comprehensive survey, stating he can only 'make notes on the regions I've been to', and in such an atomised landscape, (where many more people seem prepared to write poetry than actually buy it), it will doubtless take hindsight to distinguish the true peaks from all the false summits. Notwithstanding, *A Poetry Boom* uses a selection of eight recent anthologies to start redrawing the map, and Duncan is enjoyably partisan (of the eighty-five poets in Bloodaxe's *Identity Parade* he dismisses sixty as doing 'eloquent cover versions'). His aim is to identify the 'new sound'. The 'keys' in which it is scored ('fluffy, harlequin, unassimilated, uncoded') are anathema to the 'older poetry' with its currency of 'long-term positions [...] the theologically grounded rigour of the poet'. The new poetic 'self' is to be found in the ephemera of gesture and mannerism rather than sustained moral or ideological commitment, signalling the 'abandonment of power over situation'.

For Duncan this is democratising and mitigates against some of the unconscious literary forces at work within the last few decades. The deal with the lyric mainstream, for him, is that we're supposed to love the poet and the words are merely there to show us how. Most new poetry, consequently, is 'contemporary but not modern', and ironically its practitioners assert their individuality by deploying the same methods as thousands of others. Conversely, the process-based aesthetic of Duncan's innovators releases 'a swarm intelligence', where 'non-sequitur surprises highlight formal relationships between words', erasing any teleology from the surface of the language.

This is poetry as an enactment of its own devices, and unlike earlier avant-gardes, today's innovators are playfully committed to a 'non-narcissistic intimacy', and Duncan's paradigm is the pop song, which doesn't 'aspire to proof, but to transport via feeling, via the instantly persuasive fragments of language'.

His argument is gestural, and the difficulty remains one of capturing the whole picture. It's always easier to define a literary movement from the standpoint of a different one, and Duncan says it may be fifty years before the true nature of what we are now witnessing will become clear. The task is further complicated because anyone minded to do it must first endure the 'humiliation and numbness' of reading a lot of bad poems. His first law of Thermo-Poetics seems to be: 'Heat diffused over a large space means cold.' No sooner does one pattern of hotspots emerge than numerous exceptions suggest themselves, and any observation is obscured by the need for qualification. Undaunted, Duncan is enthusiastic in pursuit of 'proxy indicators', employing tables, lists, statistics, even faux interviews to narrow things down, before concluding that our best hope among all these little islands of poetic activity is a form of 'archipelagic fulfilment'.

Duncan's style of criticism has been described as energetic, and there are some excellent cameos here. But the energetic can also be wearying (especially at 300-plus pages), and there is a fine line between prose which is enjoyable to read, and prose which reads as though it was more enjoyable to write.

Off-white

Dominique Edde
The Crime of Jean Genet
(Seagull, 2016) £14.50

Reviewed by GREGORY WOODS

JOE ORTON and his nemesis Kenneth Halliwell used to fall about laughing at the earnestness of Jean Genet's erotic prose, apparently unaware that he too had a sense of humour. He was not writing for outsiders, nor even insider-outsiders like them. Although his publishers tended to market his books for gay readers, he said he would prefer them to fall into the hands of bankers and concierges. His filth was put on, performed for the sake of the properly shockable. (We can only guess where he'd have thought the defacing of library books came in the rank of mortal sins. Like Rimbaud, he was less interested in the sanctity of books than in the words they conveyed. He tore his favourite poems out of a borrowed Baudelaire.)

Mind you, readers of Genet have aroused enough accidental humour of their own, without his direct aid. The first essay on him I ever read (I still have my notes on it) was 'Jean Genet and the Indefensibility of Sexual Deviation' (1969), in which Philip Thody argued that 'Genet's homosexuals are unfaithful to one another because homosexuality is, of itself, a disappointing form of sexual activity'. That had the teenage me in stitches, as did his claim that Genet encourages 'the ordinary person to congratulate himself on his normality'. I'd bought four of the novels before I left school, and seen one of the plays by then, *Death Watch*, thrillingly performed in our inter-house drama competition. I did several read-throughs of *The Maids* when I was a first-year undergraduate, with a view to producing it; but in the end we failed to cast it.

Sad to say, today's bookish teenagers have no access to Thody's source of prim self-congratulation. The better-than-average branch of Waterstone's in my home city has a large Fiction department with, by British standards, a lot of translated books; but, on inspection, no Genet. None in Drama or Poetry either, but I forgot to check under Film. The local independent book shop, with far less space, did better: they had a single copy of *The Thief's Journal*, published by Faber Finds at a sturdy price of £15.

The Lebanese novelist and essayist Dominique Eddé, perhaps best known for her novel/memoir *Kite* (*Cerf-volant*, 2003), had only 'sampled' Genet's work when she first met him through the Moroccan novelist Tahar Ben Jelloun. Understandably, her main interest now is in the posthumously published *Prisoner of Love* (*Un captif amoureux*, 1986), written after he visited the Shatila refugee camp in Beirut in the aftermath of the 1982 massacre. Eddé observes that, while there are no fathers in Genet's work, all its 'real' mothers are either Arab or black. She reads him through this evident sympathy, as well as through his having read some Dostoevsky.

Eddé argues that, unlike the Russian, Genet is more interested in criminals than in their crimes, except perhaps among the counter-intuitive masculinities in *Querelle of Brest*. 'Murderer' may be a moral and erotic status, but the act that earned it is of marginal significance. A man whose favourite word (who among writers has a favourite word?) she says was *délicatesse* 'embodies the difference between shame and guilt'. Genet's shame, she explains, 'does not answer to men but to a higher idea: to God or to gods [...]. Having left the judgement of men behind, his stain belongs to him alone, it is *pure*'. In this respect, 'he represents an inversion of the Dostoevskian character, where shame gives rise to guilt and guilt gives rise to shame'.

The other figure in Eddé's discussion is Nietzsche: 'the same rejection of morality [...] the same inversion of values, the same mockery, the same demolition of monotheistic religion [...] the same love for the Greeks and Dionysus'. But the more she lists, the less like Nietzsche Genet seems.

Eddé operates within a pretty short attention span. I was distracted from her book's whole by the oddity of its parts. For a while she gets bogged down in his excremental interests. 'As for the little kingdom of the wc, no one has said more about it than him, or said it better' is a coy way of putting it (I wonder how the original French goes), and the tweeness of that 'little kingdom' comes far short of the beshitted universe mapped out in Genet's prose. I would suggest that Pierre Guyotat has a lot more to say on excrement than Genet – but let it pass.

My gob was more resoundingly smacked when, after stating that Genet's father was called Blanc (which Genet himself didn't know), Eddé takes an airy ramble through the various uses of the word 'blanc' in his books, eventually traipsing into the fact (which, likewise, he never knew) that he would end up with a biographer called White (Edmund of that ilk).

An Essential Addition

Roger Scruton
The Ring of Truth: The Wisdom of Wagner's 'Ring of the Nibelung'
(Allen Lane, 2016) £25.00

Reviewed by ROGER CALDWELL

WAGNER IS PRESENT in *The Waste Land* in the form of two pregnant snippets from *Tristan and Isolde* and in the glossolalia, intermediate between speech and music, of the Rhinemaidens. It is hard, nonetheless, to imagine him as a poet in his own right – the texts that make up *The Ring of the Nibelung* are now inseparable from the music that was to accompany them. Yet it was as a dramatic poem, privately printed, that they were first presented to the world – when not a note of the music had yet been written. Remarkably, in the four years that he worked on them, so engrossed was he in the drama that evolved before his eyes that he virtually ceased to compose music.

There was no mystery about why Wagner turned to the sort of literary materials that he did. A mythology was needed for his great design, and researching the remains of the old pagan culture was an essential part of what it was to belong to the nationalistic Young Germany movement. But compiling the text of *The Ring* involved no straightforward taking-over of a ready-made mythology. Certainly he took a little from the Nibelungenlied, and rather more from the Icelandic Volsung Saga, but he drew as much from the Eddas, developing hints in the obscurest corners of the literature that he was able to interpret for his own purposes. It was as if he already knew – in an inchoate fashion – what he wanted to say, and was able to re-invent a mythology now only surviving in fragments. Certainly the Norse religion with its concept of Ragnarök, in which the doom of the gods is fated, was germane to the purpose of the young revolutionary who in 1848 manned the barricades of Dresden along with Bakunin, intent on overturning the old political (and religious) order for ever. Of course, by the time he had completed the composition of *Götterdämmerung,* the last opera of the cycle, he was neither young nor an active political revolutionary, but the text he set was substantially the same as that which he had originally written. He was now a follower of Schopenhauer, for whom the only solution to the torment of existence lay in the setting aside of the will, in renunciation. In the original wording we are promised that, with the departure of the gods, a future society of love is in the offing. This promise is now omitted: the cycle ends in a resigned acceptance of fate rather than in the triumph of a revolution in which the gods had been ousted by mankind. In Scruton's account Wagner had come to see that 'the socialist dreams were every bit as illusory as the religion they had set out to replace'.

Wagner's text started with a poem on the death of Siegfried. This he found didn't fully make sense in itself and needed an introduction which in turn required further introductions. The text was thus, as it were, written backwards. Composition of the music, however, proceeded forwards, so that the last texts to be written were the first to receive musical treatment. Given the length of time it took to compete the cycle – there is an amazing twelve-year gap between the second and third acts of *Siegfried* – it would not be surprising for there to be inconsistencies of style and substance. What *is* surprising is that they are so few. Wagner's views on the relation between words and music had changed in the course of composition. Whereas in *Der Reingold* the music is subservient to the requirements of the words, by the time of *Götterdämmerung* the music tells the story as much as the words do – much of the drama is now enacted through the orchestra alone. In many places words have become superfluous. The system of leitmotifs makes for an ever-growing complexity of effect: it works by association, in that for each new situation in which a leitmotif occurs we are reminded of previous such situations, so that there is an accumulation of meaning, an ever-greater richesse of thoughts and emotions. Scruton in an appendix lists no fewer than 180 leitmotifs, though he admits that some of them are questionable; in this, as is so often the case with Wagner, much depends on who is doing the counting.

It is easy to forget, now that his writings are little read – except maybe to mine them for evidence of his anti-Semitism – how influential they were. Wagner was a formidable theoretician with a wide-ranging, if eclectic, mind: it was through his prose as much as his music that he exercised an influence on the symbolists. He was deeply versed in philosophy: his conversion from a Left Hegelian position to an immersion in Schopenhauer is delineated most fully in Brian Magee's magnificent *Wagner and Philosophy* (2000) to which Scruton's book may be seen as complementary. The ambitions of *The Ring* are immense: there is a sense in which it is a history of the world, despite the relatively small number of characters and locales it presents. If the subject-matter is largely drawn from Norse mythology, other traditions keep breaking through. It is impossible to hear the bickerings between Wotan and Fricka without being reminded of similar exchanges between Zeus and Hera in Homer. In his role as law-giver and his ruling by covenant or treaty, he is akin to the God of the Old Testament. Most often we see him as an Odin figure, the wanderer, always bearing his spear and wearing a wide-brimmed hat covering his missing eye. (Wotan is the one character to appear in all four of the operas, but we are only told how he lost it – parenthetically and less than fully – in the final opera of the cycle.) Siegfried, by contrast, is in some respects a figure out of the *Märchenzeit* or time of fairy-tales, living deep in the forest, coming to understand the songs of the birds, seeking in vain to understand what fear is. He is, many feel, an unsatisfactory hero, the radiant boy behaving most often like a churlish adolescent and being something of a *Dummlkopf*: even his love for Brünnhilde hardly redeems him, as he all too easily falls into the trap laid for him by Hagen to betray her. It is Brünnhilde herself who has the truly heroic part, her self-immolation being, for Wotan, the deed that will redeem the world.

Quite what that redemption amounts to is a matter for controversy. Interpretations of *The Ring* have been many and varied. A Marxist interpretation (such as Bernard Shaw's) is not to be easily dismissed: it is not for nothing that Marx and Wagner were contemporaries. Nibelheim, for example, under the tyrannous rule of Alberich, is surely an image of industrial production in early capitalism, and Siegfried's forging of the sword Nothung can be seen as joyous self-expression, work free of alienation. But one may wonder if any single interpretation is possible of a work so vast and with such a density of ideation behind it, and one that took decades to complete. Bryan Magee holds that there is no single level on which it can be consistently interpreted. This is true, I think, to the experience of the listener: the work is always locally intelligible, but it is difficult at any point to keep in mind while listening to a particular passage the full significance of its place in the whole. Scruton protests against 'reductive' interpretations, but when he solemnly tells us that Wotan's spear 'succinctly summarises Hegel's view of the state' one might well wonder if it does and, if so, whether that is what it *essentially* does. At various points he tells us that central to *The Ring* is the emergence of the free individual from the natural order, the incompatibility of love and power, the dependence of the legal order on the machinery of production and exchange, and the need to regard certain aspects of life as sacred. Surely all those themes are present. But, if so many themes are to be seen as central, it is hard to see how the centre can hold. Not that sheer anarchy takes over, but rather that there is no centre to begin with. It is also noticeable that the themes that Scruton most emphasises in Wagner are themes that have figured largely in Scruton's own philosophical books of the last three decades, and the wisdom that Wagner is said to offer is as much his own. There is undoubtedly an element here of Scruton seeing Wagner in his own image. But Wagner's work is such that it rather invites us to do so. In a ninety-page chapter Scruton recounts the story that is told in *The Ring*, but even the simple telling of the story brings with it a degree of interpretation, and one suspects that no two people, if called on to do so, would tell the story in the same way.

Wagner is unsurpassed in presenting an originary Edenic world of nature, in evoking in music a sort of time before time. For the German prefix 'Ur' there is no equivalent in English. It is this antediluvian world (*Urwelt*) that haunts *The Ring*. It is the primeval forest (*Urwald*) in which Siegfried lives where he hears the forest murmurings, understands the songs of the birds, and tries to learn what fear is. The rule of Wotan, by law and treaty, brings order, but also the loss of this originary world. The new order itself, however, is unsustainable, and Wotan is a deeply divided figure: if he himself is 'nothing without the law' he also loves his progeny who transgress it. The ecstatic love between Siegmund and Sieglinde Fricka finds shocking and unlawful – clearly it is one unacceptable to an ordered society – but Wotan condones, even celebrates it. So, it must be said, does the music. There is a sense in which Scruton tries to normalise Wagner, but Wagner in the end is resistant to normalisation. For Hegel, as Scruton reminds us, public morality is the final court of moral appeal. But for Wagner there is a higher court than public morality – the erotic love he portrays is not reconcilable with, and has no respect for, bourgeois society, but is excessive: it transcends all rules. Wagner remains a revolutionary of sorts – and not just in musical terms – to the end.

Scruton's book, nonetheless, is an essential addition to the (extensive) Wagner literature. He is patient and level-headed in assessing the contributions of previous commentators on Wagner, some of which, by any standards, are cranky, and is a master, as always, in explaining complex ideas. There is much useful musicological analysis. No one will agree with everything he says, but everyone – not only Wagnerian neophytes – will have something to learn from it. It is also, clearly, a labour of love. Wagner himself would surely have approved.

unlike Heaney, he is never even quietly flashy.

An Emeritus Fellow of Wadham College, where he taught medieval English, it's hardly surprising that O'Donoghue's poems reach out to Pindar and Ovid, Dante and the Gawain poet. What *is* surprising is that he does so without them feeling self-consciously literary. In 'Procne', for instance, we visit Queen Gunnhild and a matchmaking Pandarus before we even get to the Procne of the title. This could feel like a highbrow display, but 'Procne' (and poems like it), is so at home with the everyday – with the return of a swallow – that each reference feels of a piece with the 'rusting galvanise' of the poet's shed.

Not every poem in *The Seasons of Cullen Church* is a success. 'Stigma', for instance, fizzles out in the last line as the poet goes from the poverty of his childhood to asylum seekers 'drowning / in their hundreds in the Med'. O'Donoghue's awareness of the danger of nostalgia is characteristically generous, but in this case it is a loss for the poem.

But so many are a success. 'The Will', 'Ballybeg Priory' and 'The Din Beags' bring together, without comment, 'the grimness and awful untouchable sadness of things' with life's tenderness and delight. Cruelty exists alongside admiration ('And Spoil a Child'); humour is set next to sadism ('Robbing the Orchard'); the tragedy of the strong man at a circus in 'Sawdust' – wrapped in a 'starry blanket' then hurried away before the children are given 'buns to hold out for the elephants' – is almost unbearably poignant. I didn't have a rural Irish Catholic upbringing but the title poem almost made me believe I did. The balance of qualities in O'Donoghue's poetry – humility, sweet-spokeness, tragedy, wistfulness, humour – combine to create a quiet majesty.

Buns for
the Elephants

Bernard O'Donoghue
The Seasons of Cullen Church
(Faber & Faber, 2016) £12.99

Reviewed by MAITREYABANDHU

RANDALL JARRELL REMARKED of Robert Frost's poems how little they seem 'performances', and how much they were instead 'things made of lives and the world that the lives inhabit'. I felt the same about Bernard O'Donoghue's new collection, *The Seasons of Cullen Church*. When so much modern poetry seems like a performance, or else the latest instalment from the School of Nice Feelings, O'Donoghue's poems are an object lesson in how to write poetry that matters. The new collection confirms him as one of the most lyrical, amused, tragic and serious poets currently writing in English.

On first reading, the poems seem almost studiedly commonplace, as if the writer is hardly writing poetry at all. They have the immediacy of a story told over a Guinness, a joke heard on a train. And yet each poem keeps you on your toes just enough: not enough to cause strain, but enough to keep you alert to syntax that mimics everyday speech but heightens it, ever so slightly, into poetry. Syntax and word choice stay just the right side of surprising, without drawing attention to the poet's scrupulousness. Like Seamus Heaney, O'Donoghue has a 'reluctance to be grand';

The brightness
between trees

Fiona Sampson, *The Catch*
(Chatto & Windus, 2016) £10

Reviewed by SUE LEIGH

THE TITLE OF Fiona Sampson's latest collection, *The Catch*, comes from an old word for a round song, one that keeps going and that you may join in with, if you wish. Many of the poems in the book are songs – praise songs – for creatures, the land, people, lived moments. They have been inspired by time spent in France, the natural environment and what Sampson herself describes as 'that most difficult of experiences to evoke, happiness'. It is a tender book, curious, sensuous, full of light.

The Catch represents a real process of searching, of finding new ways of doing and saying things. The poems frequently inhabit marginal places – memory, imagination, dream – encountered at early morning or evening. The book opens with 'Wake' where first light is 'a slim cat / coming home through Top Field' and closes with a child in bed, the shadows meeting across the grass 'to swallow time / the light put out / in each grass stalk'. 'The Border' describes a night drive in which creatures surface from a deep dream state to reveal themselves on the road – and haven't you also, asks the speaker, 'arrived / once again at / astonishment / at the brink of dream?'

The poet invites us to regain the way of looking we had as a child – to hear 'the wind / along the pavement / wind shaking the hedge and the cherry branches'. Moments of recognition, connection, small epiphanies are celebrated – the sound of doves on waking, wet sheets on a clothesline, an early morning encounter with horses. In 'Daily Bread' a cup of coffee taken to a window seat, the woodwork shining in the morning light, reveals 'how you're alive and how you live'. We would do well to recognise these moments for what they are, the poems seem to say, to try not to possess them.

Sampson is interested in pushing at boundaries – not only of feeling and consciousness but also of form. Many of the poems consist of a single sentence with minimal punctuation and are shaped by what the poet describes as a 'push-me-pull-you rhythm of line breaks and stanza breaks'. So despite the apparent simplicity and the lack of detailed description, the syntax intrigues, we must slow down, read with more attention, be alert to possibilities.

Alongside love and illumination there is a counterweight – 'the troubled wind' that blows through the trees in 'Stone Fruit', 'speaking the word *loss*'; the stag that knows 'he carries death / in his green antlers'. A group of poems about sickness and disease remind us, as the speaker says in 'Insulin', that 'The human body is a heavy machine. / Such stillness / when the motor shudders and stops.' And always there is an awareness of time, its passing.

'Really what I want', the speaker says in 'Stone House', a poem in the final section of the book, is to go back to 'a source / that's inexhaustible / and daily [...] I mean a wall / warm with the sun thick with it / like shelter / a wall thickly curved / and made by hands / whose gestures I could make / in my turn'.

A Way

Laozi (trans. Martyn Crucefix)
Daodejing
(Enitharmon Press, 2016) £9.99

Reviewed by SHENGCHI HSU

LAOZI'S *DAODEJING* (or Lao Tzu's *Tao Te Ching*) is one of the best-known Chinese classics in the West. Written using five thousand Chinese characters, *Daodejing* is composed of two sections with a total of eighty-one chapters. The book sets out to explain the philosophy of *Dao* through a variety of juxtaposed examples *Laozi* observed in nature. This philosophy later provided the founding principles of Taoism. The text owes some of its popularity to Winnie-the-Pooh and his adoption of *Tao* as a way to demonstrate his life's philosophy. It is not uncommon for readers of *Daodejing* to take the text purely as a philosophical and spiritual guide to life. What is rarely discussed in academia or in public is the literary value of the text.

Laozi's sophisticated literary techniques are clear: he uses neat paralleled rhymed verses, repetition, metaphors, and vivid images drawn from everyday objects to convey his thinking. The Chinese language's tonal system adds to the musicality and pace of these verses. Given the literariness in *Daodejing*, and the difficulty in deciphering ancient Chinese texts' economical diction, translating Laozi's philosophy and poetics into languages distant from the Chinese language system poses real challenges to translators.

These challenges have not deterred translators from producing new translations; a simple search discloses more than a thousand versions available to readers, ranging from Arthur Waley's translation in 1934 to the *New York Times* best-selling translation by Stephen Mitchell.

Martyn Crucefix follows in the footsteps of these translators to produce his new 'versions' of *Daodejing*. By calling his work a 'new version', Crucefix acknowledges his debt to the works of his predecessors and insists that his interpretation is a different one. The Introduction to the collection begins with a brief overview of the Chinese original. Archaeological discoveries continue to uncover fragments of versions of *Daodejing* from different ancient dynasties. Which version should he follow? This question opens a space for the poet to exercise his creative imagination, listening to Laozi's teaching and reflecting on it. Crucefix transposes Laozi into the Western contemporary as a teacher who speaks a modern English vernacular to probe the unnameable Dao and its manifestation. Each poem is given a title to guide readers on the journey of realisation.

The poems begin with a long dash to suggest the effect of speech associated with the Chinese classics. Crucefix abandons rhymed verse and arranges the spoken words in unrhymed, unmetred free verse. To compensate for the loss of end rhyme, he makes frequent use of alliteration and internal rhymes to generate pace, texture and musicality. His arrangement of sounds entails repeating words and paralleling syntactical structures to evoke a feeling that these verses function as a rhetorical vortex. This feeling is enhanced by the absence of punctuation to mark pauses and sentence breaks. This strategy underlines the antiquity of the ancient text where punctuation was not used; but at the same time it challenges the reader's grasp of Laozi's philosophy, creating unnecessary syntactical obscurity. If the poet intends contemporary readers to appreciate *Daodejing* through his language, then his deliberately unpunctuated lines increase the mythical aspect of the text, at the same time encouraging readers to hear the words and experience the paradoxes the world presents through the irreconcilable syntax.

Crucefix captures the spirit of Laozi's philosophical

inquiry through a poetics of 'indirect direction' that speaks in a transparent yet seemingly solid way. Language is imperfect, and languages present different world views. Crucefix's Laozi overcomes some of the unresolvable differences inherent in languages and offers *another* way into the mysterious Dao.

The Way

John McAuliffe, *The Way In*
(The Gallery Press, 2015) £9.00

Reviewed by HILARY DAVIES

THE TITLE POEM of John McAuliffe's most recent collection, *The Way In*, closes with the line, 'The door, the boat, the way out the only way in'. Doors and boats figure prominently in this volume, which is surely fitting for someone whose professional career as a writer has meant regular shuttling between Ireland and mainland Britain. It makes for an itinerant existence, at once exciting and, in both senses, unsettling. The train journey to and from Holyhead is one of the threads that gives continuity in these poems, 'the train that [...] / runs between like a thought, // a thought with rain streaking it / and fields like a faithful companion.' Yet there is also a sense of tensions set up: good tensions where absence makes the heart grow fonder, 'the gulls flying up out of the thought / that I go away to hear you say my name'. But other tensions crowd in too: in 'Echo', the poet returns from a stay in Lisbon to find he has lost his key, his home altered, indifferent to him, running its life independently, making him feel somehow superfluous to requirements, 'getting a laugh from knocking on my own door, / but not so much when / [...] it sounds, on the other side, / [...] as if I've been, these many days, an echo // right here really, of a life that has gone on, regardless'.

McAuliffe's own clear point of departure and return remains, nevertheless, his native Ireland. He explores this in the central sequence, 'Home Again'. The book's cover tells us that McAuliffe has borrowed the form of Edmund Spenser's famous satire-pastoral, 'Colin Clout's Come Home Again'. Yet it is difficult to see how this works in practice. Certainly the first poem, 'The Red Lion', which takes place in a pub where members of an informal poetry workshop have gathered, has a vague echo of Clout's assembly of shepherds eager for news of what the great Queen Cynthia's court is like. But Spenser's bucolic bard relates exclusively his journey to, sojourn in and impressions of (we must understand it) England. He concerns himself with the strangeness and wonder of it all, doling out praise or criticism for other poets, professing his admiration for Cynthia and love for his chosen lady, Rosalinde, ending with an unexpected and beautiful vision of cosmic and human love. McAuliffe's sequence takes place largely in Ireland; there are poems that talk about pagan ritual, the ruination of Ascendancy 'big houses' (a swipe at Spenser), unearthed gold chalices, and ancient hurts. But also Manchester and Mill Hill, signposts to the poet's personal experience as an Irish emigrant to the mainland. The link to Spenser remains tenuous: the poem 'Colin, Again', in which McAuliffe seems to yoke a discussion of the power of poetry to Spenser's vision, undercuts the Elizabethan with its scare quotation marks and throwaway last line, 'the other world that is not all it's cut out to be...' As to the question of form, there is little hint, in McAuliffe's long, loose syntax and noticeable reliance on the present participle, of Spenser's question and answer structure and tightly rhymed prosody. 'Home Again', surely, asks to be read on its own merits.

Hilarious & Sad

James Tate, *Dome of the Hidden Pavilion*
(Harper Collins, 2016) £13.50;
Em Strang, *Bird-Woman*
(Shearsman, 2016) £8.95

Reviewed by IAN SEED

Dome of the Hidden Pavilion was James Tate's seventeenth and last book of poetry. It was published shortly after his death in 2015. Tate had a long and distinguished career, although his work is not that well-known in the UK. His first collection, *The Lost Pilot* (1967), was selected by Dudley Fitts for the Yale Series of Younger Poets. His *Selected Poems* (published in the UK by Carcanet) won the Pulitzer Prize and the William Carlos Williams Award in 1991.

Influenced by Wallace Stevens, many of Tate's earlier poems use unrhymed tercets and adopt a reflective, meditative tone. They are haunted by a sense of loss, as shown in one of his more familiar poems, 'The Lost Pilot', written for his father who was killed in action in 1944:

I feel dead. I feel as if I were
the residue of a stranger's life,
that I should pursue you.

My head cocked toward the sky,
I cannot get off the ground,
and, you, passing over again,

fast, perfect, and unwilling
to tell me that you are doing
well, or that it was mistake

that placed you in that world,
and me in this; or that misfortune
placed these worlds in us.

From his second collection, *The Oblivion Ha-Ha* (1970), until the late 1980s, Tate's poems moved to a highly original use of surrealism and absurdism, with, in the words of Anthony Caleshu, a close attention to 'language games, syntactical variations, and shifting registers' (see 'James Tate's Recent Prose Poetry' in *PNR* 205). These poems are often funny enough to make one laugh out loud, but they could also be powerfully poignant. In an interview with Charles Simic for the *Paris Review* in 2006, Tate himself said: 'I love my funny poems, but I'd rather break your heart. And if I can do both in the same poem, that's the best. If you laughed earlier in the poem, and I bring you close to tears in the end, that's the best. That's most rewarding for you and for me too.'

With the publication of *Distance from Loved Ones* in 1990 there was a distinct move away from compression to a more open narrative which makes use of the longer line and enjambment. Although the poems are still very much in the absurdist tradition, they rely mainly on the twists and turns of a storyline. Although they do not look like prose poems because they are not square blocks of text on page, the effect they have is one not dissimilar to that of the prose poems of Max Jacob. Tate, like Jacob, draws us irresistibly into another world.

Dome of the Hidden Pavilion continues in this vein. The only real difference is that the lines now come so close to the right margin of the page that they look tantalisingly like prose with a ragged right margin. From the opening lines of the first poem, 'Mr Leaves', this is a book which, like any collection of good stories, is hard to put down:

I saw someone coming in the distance, but couldn't make out who it was. The closer they got the more blurred the face became. Until finally I saw it was just a whirlwind of leaves. It was only me on a football field walking toward the street with my handbag thrown over my shoulder with this big funnel of leaves coming toward me like a man. Then it passed by me and went on up the street. And then it disappeared. I walked on, toward the bank where I had some business to do.

Most of the poem-stories in *The Dome of the Hidden Pavilion* feature first-person narrators in small-town America who are simply trying to get on with the daily business of living when something strange and out-of-this-world enters their lives. There are subtle religious connotations here, and it is difficult at times not to think of Tate as a kind of secular George Herbert. If only there could be an honest meeting, then perhaps some kind of healing towards wholeness could occur. However, in the world depicted by Tate many of these meetings with strangers seem to dissolve before they have really taken place. The effect is both hilarious and sad, and however outlandish the story, the moment of epiphany (usually one of realisation of failure) feels authentic and somehow inevitable.

There is a great emphasis on dialogue in these poems. The frequent repetition of 'I said', 'he said' and 'she said' has a rhythmical, even hypnotic effect. Yet, as in an Ionesco play, the characters are mainly talking at cross-purposes, frequently in a mechanical manner, as if they are speaking only as they are expected to because of the way they are trapped, for example by a marital relationship:

My wife said to me, 'Leroy, if you want rabbit stew you're just going to have to go out there and kill a rabbit.' I said, 'I never said anything about wanting rabbit stew.' 'But you were acting like you wanted rabbit stew,' she said. 'I don't know what you mean by that. I was just being me,' I said.
('The Rabbit God')

One could easily imagine cartoon illustrations with these poems, but as with many cartoons, there is often a more serious political purpose at work, even within the most slapstick of these pieces. Although Tate never takes an explicit political stance, the effect of politics can be seen in his characters' lack of control over their own destiny, which is decided by much greater events such as war and acts (or feared acts) of terrorism. An existential terror of the abyss lies beneath the surface of all these poems, however comically it is portrayed:

         'I walk around all day feeling
there is something missing. I don't know what it is, but
    nothing
seems complete without it. Even when my husband's here,
    I feel
it, some crack in the fabric of our being. Do you know what
that's called?' she said. 'Everything is in here,' I said.
'Like right now,' she said. 'I feel that God has flown away [...]'
('The Encyclopedia Salesman')

¶ *Bird-Woman* is Em Strang's first collection of poetry. In its powerfully-meditative tone, its striking and compelling imagery, and its depiction of another world which nevertheless is inextricably linked to everyday reality, it bears a resemblance to James Tate's work. Here we are in the presence of the mythical, but the myth is embedded in a very physical way to the real landscape of the Scottish hills and forests. At the same time, this landscape is forever shifting and may dissolve into something more terrifyingly metaphysical and dreamlike, a place

where great northern divers
are throats from the other side,
where nothing any of us can speak of
seems real
(from 'Apokatastasis')

Beauty is ever-present and yet along with that beauty there is a sense of menace, which may turn unexpectedly at any moment into devastating violence:

The two men, hands in pockets,
feet sinking into the grey-black of the road.
The sun is hot and high and they wade into the field,
lose themselves to the waist in straight, green blades.

The bird-woman is scuffing the soft, loose earth,
making a bowl for the body.

She lays the bird with its broken neck
and covers it with clover,
small red flowers, lucky leaves.

When the men capsize her
the pleats of her dress unfurl.

The ground takes their weight.

('Bird-Woman')

Strang's narratives play with ambiguity. We can
never be quite sure what is going on, what has really
happened. It is as if we have caught a glimpse of
something, only to look again to see that nothing is
there, or that it is not what we thought it was. The
differences between animals and human beings (or
whatever we imagine those differences to be) dissolve
into one another. Our ability to be at one with other
animals is rooted in physicality, yet it also has a
strong mystical dimension, one that may be terrifying
but that will ultimately enrich us if we can allow what
is 'other' to enter our lives. In this sense, Strang is a
less despairing poet than Tate because she believes,
ultimately, that meaningful encounters can and must
take place.

The dramatic (and at times tragic) in Strang's work
is fortunately counterbalanced in many poems by a
gentle humour and the affectionate portraits of char-
acters who inhabit the landscape, for example 'Tog
Muhoni', reminiscent of Edward Thomas's 'Lob':

Because when you see him you know, small light in a night
    forest,
that his name is Tog Muhoni and his smile tells the way the
    river bends
and how he crossed it, one foot dragging behind like a
    snapped limb:

to stay or to go? You're late for something, driving, and your
    whole life
is mapped out in the arm he's missing.

(from 'Tog Muhoni')

As with Tate, it is impossible not to want to read
on. *Bird-Woman* is a powerful first collection whose
poems enter the bloodstream and remain.

Sexting Dionysus

Elsa Cross (trans. Anamaria Crowe
Serrano), *Beyond the Sea* (£10.95);
Sandeep Parmar, *Eidolon* (£8.95);
Linda Black, *Slant* (£9.95);
Em Strang, *Bird-Woman* (£9.95)
Susan Connolly, *Bridge of the Ford*
(£10.95) (all Shearsman)

Reviewed by JOHN MUCKLE

SHEARSMAN'S WOMEN POETS tend to be in a
modernist line, but the eclecticism and range of this
international list makes for a sense of many voices
and cultural locations rather than a unified academic
feminism. Elsa Cross is a Mexican poet, once strongly
praised by Octavio Paz, who writes sequences which
have a diaphanous sheen, and a sort of limpidity:
they are 'poetic', 'feminine', sonorous in Spanish and
light and precise in a fine translation. The adjoining
islands of *Beyond the Sea* are governed respectively
by Apollo and Dionysus, the poems of each section
composed in traditional dithyrambs and odes. The
ode is her mode: Homeric voyagings, meetings at
which lovers combust into white incandescence, as
their eternal essences airily permute and conjoin.
Her manner is vatic, oracular, and her breadth of
imagination considerable. The first sequence, of three
odes, begins with 'Stones', the birth of cities and the
ruins of cities built on utterance, on prophecies:

The sun lashes, naked, on marble.
Inscriptions
wide and light its messages:
letters like porticos,
triglyphs,
            vibrant propyleums –
and just where names and things collide
veins open in the marble
                    like entries to other dreams.

('Stones')

Her schema unfolds into 'Waves', a lazily sensual
poem with the blue Aegean gently slapping at its
rump, far richer in description and human life, and
finally 'Cicadas' in which the intoxications of land-
scape and love and myth are fused and the winged
god finally appears:

Unfolding in my hands I see
                the creatures of dreams
but don't know what is engendered
between my steps
                and the rocks sinking their sharp edges
                into my feet,
between my eyes
                and the faded mosaics
– winged Dionysus on his panther.

('Cicadas')

The remaining and larger part of *Beyond the Sea* is in
classical dithyrambs, addressed to a lover, to the dark
gods of two cultures, and it's all deeply saturated in
the honeyed light of the Greek islands, fusing longing
and the calling up of cultural ghosts; Cross's poems
are explosive, carefully set charges, poetic nitroglyc-
erine to blow the living gods out of ancient rock.

¶ Sandeep Parmar's *Eidolon* visits some of the same
places as Cross's *Beyond the Sea*, but in a different
mode and through a more recognisably modern, or at
least Anglo-American, feminist cultural perspective,
exploring the Helen myth via her status as an eidolon,
'fixed yet unfixed' (Whitman, 'Eidolons'): false-image,
idea, demi-goddess, cultural sign (dreaded word:
icon) or emblem of destructive female beauty, polit-
ical intriguing and treachery. Parmar's Helen is a
modern woman, sexting her dates and protesting her
innocence; but this is no cheap modern knock-off of

a classical myth, instead it is a delicate and insightful exploration of women's status in the ancient world, the construction of an enduring female archetype, its over-turning, and a sequence of love poems in a beautiful and evocative open-form, projective verse, to women surviving in the aftermath of these myths, floating in an air of disconnection. I can't believe how well this long poem works, shimmering and darting forwards, glittering with linguistic jewels, bristling with insight:

Helen, dispirited
    camera-bound   Helen
fetching the paper from the front lawn in her dressing gown
a lot of the time
and knowing when the phone will ring
seconds before   by the click of its current

¶ Linda Black is also a storytelling poet, but an oblique one. *Slant* refers to Emily Dickinson ('Tell all the Truth but tell it slant'), but Black's hesitant, unclosed narratives and heart-stopping pauses are more reminiscent of the late Lee Harwood's poetry: crystalline, fictive, artful. Her vocabulary is more recherche than Harwood's, her poems often more tautly constructed, more pictorial. In her lusher moments she can disappear into lists of fanciful compound words and sonic pairings, although it is in and through these devices that her poetry achieves its rich, sing-song music; but there are 'little gregarious footings' (to quote the poet in 'She takes herself out of herself') whereby her poems gain purchase on a human story and haul themselves up and out into shared experience and the quotidian.

Up & down stairs   in & out
the washing machine   has become
where she is   where the moon got her
She has nowhere   goes by foot
tripping over her own   worse for wear
explains nothing   doesn't admit   she is not
of that faith   It is many years ago now
she turned   walked away   no thought
from her own good   someone else's
consequence   & the madman   inside
where ten pinafores hang
('She walks for days')

Her assemblages from Virginia Woolf and John Ruskin (in 'At the little deal table under the lamp' and 'The seven lamps') are highly effective, but it is a bit like shooting fish in a barrel to make some-thing good out of these sources, and it is in her own searching, slanted stories that Black's poetic gift shines, in her inventive use of nursery rhyme and old vernaculars, in her recognition that 'bread needs the tin of strife' ('There is little tonight for supper' p 88).
¶ Em Strang's strong first collection is satisfying in a different way. Many of these poems are spells or charms that conjure with the textures and rhythms of Scottish rural life. Taciturn men walk in smelling of rutting stag, turn up to take down the barbed wire fence around the second pasture and disappear never to be seen again, a bird-woman and a bird-house attain mythic dream-status, magnificent horses nose in from all directions, and women's lives on

the land are deeply explored and usually celebrated in many of these beautifully honed poems. Strang has a real gift for myth, dream, ritual, the eternal return, for repetition and latent history in this observant and keenly intelligent book; some might find her subject-matter parochial, but through it she reaches out for a global sense of where we are now.

When the hunger is here and the anger
there's no room for the necessity of grief
and the small bird of the body
stabs it beak into the day again and again,
like a robot working a conveyor belt;
and all sense of faith is lost in an endless flight
from the soft feathers of the self,
from one timeless embodied life to another [...]
('When the Hunger is Here and the Anger')

¶ Susan Connolly's *The Bridge of the Ford: Visual Poetry from Drogheda* is an agreeable collection of *poesie concret*, taking its bearings from Edwin Morgan, Dom Sylvester Houedard, Ian Hamilton Finlay and the Canadian poet bP Nichol. There are two circular love mandalas, some austere grids, rows of medieval tiles, pieces evoking embroideries, boats sailing across harbours, grained lists of local street names, a reverence for the Book of Kells and a number striking political pieces, cairns or charms for the release of imprisoned aid workers. Some of these poems are mainly concerned with visual texture, but many of them memorialise a shared experience of something in nature, elevating a moment's communion into a rare and exquisite kind of love poetry, such as the first poem in the book, 'Winter Solstice at Dowth, 3 pm'. Connolly's take on visual poetry is delicate, well thought out, her own.

Is there a universal poetic consensus on how writing is gendered? Hardly. But all these poets do share a preoccupation with certain modalities of care – whether sexual or bodily in a wider sense, domestic or mystical, political or natural – that slant to the articulation of emotion and its consequences, offer in some sense a shared female experience, and all are strongly drawn to mythopoeia, and to the ancient world – whether Greek, Mayan, Paleolithic or Celtic – with a vertical and active way of seeing the past in the present that recalls their modernist forebears.

More of the World

Stephen Burt
The Poem is You: 60 Contemporary Poems and How to Read Them
(Belknap Press, 2016) $27.95

Reviewed by HENRY KING

STEPH BURT PLAYS a particular role in the network of contemporary poetry: in addition to writing poems and more traditional scholarly work as Professor of Poetry at Harvard University (especially on Randall

Jarrell), Burt is one of the most popularisers of others' work. *The Poem is You* follows 2009's *Close Calls with Nonsense*, making the format of an anthology of poems with a critical essay something of a personal hallmark. The mission is evangelical and educative: yes, contemporary poetry can be daunting, both in its forms and range of cultural references, but it is navigable with a conscientious guide. The presentation of *The Poem Is You* is even more inviting than *Close Calls*: the second-person pronoun in the title (taken from the John Ashbery poem with which the selection begins) suggests intimacy, perhaps promising to give as much attention to the reader as the texts; and the subtitle, *60 Contemporary Poems and How to Read Them*, is less austere, more encouraging that that of *Close Calls with Nonsense: Reading New Poetry*.

It's sometimes a cheap shot to discuss the introduction to an anthology at length, but the essay that introduces *The Poem Is You* is intrinsically interesting. Burt points out that:

the best introductions to poetry in general spend much of their time, quite rightly, on poets such as Shakespeare and Emily Dickinson [...] rather than focusing only on recent decades.

That's where this book comes in. And yet any approach to recent American poetry as a whole—even this one—raises the problems it tries to solve, much like any attempt to see the United States of America.

The problem itself is quintessentially American, going back to Walt Whitman's desire to bring every aspect of America within their democratic vision. Burt even adopts a Whitmanian rhetoric of exhaustive inclusivity:

Here you'll find mothers, fathers, lovers, friends, painters, marine biologists, soldiers, horses, foresters, goths, teachers, teens, post-Marxist saxophonists, more horses, beauty contestants, prophetic undead pianists, and kinds of kinky sex; you'll encounter slices of life in modern cities, defenses of bourgeois suburbia, and more than one elaborate jeremiad against how we treat our earth, water and air.

But of course, nobody can be completely inclusive: Burt admits that

I was slightly surprised, by the end of the selection process, at the ratio of so-called lyric to anti-lyric poems, at how many of the recent poems I chose to include had consistent scenes, and speakers and senses of voice: readers attached to the present-day post-avant-garde may find in this book, not a case against it, but a claim that it's not the only game in town.

I find that slight surprise itself slightly surprising: Burt has always tended more towards the tradition represented in poets such as Randall Jarrell and, through Jarrell, W. H. Auden, than the aggressively experimental. Nevertheless, Burt has omnivorous taste and a voracious appetite: there can be few critics better suited to approaching, at least, that stance of Whitmanian inclusiveness, both of the level of poetic form and individual/group identities.

This vision is even more salutary in a book published in 2016, when scapegoating and bigotry dominated American political discourse. Burt's credo is that '[n]o matter how you describe yourself, you can get more wisdom, more grace, and more of the world if you look beyond your own experience, as well as looking for it, in what you read.' This makes *The Poem Is You* an inquisitive and humane book, in a way that now looks like a small act of political resistance. Burt claims poetry can do two things better than just about any other medium: poems 'let us imagine some else's interior life, almost as if it were or could have been ours', and they 'keep us alert to the social, political, and economic problems that make the world worse than it could be'. Both of these tasks will be imperative in the next four (or even more) years.

The sheer number of flourishing poetic scenes and traditions in America today makes for a bewildering spectacle, at least for anyone who cannot dedicate themselves to keeping tabs with every development; in fact reading *The Poem Is You* can be quite a humbling experience, as one realises how limited one's own perspective on contemporary poetry is. This range, and Burt's impressive knowledge of and sympathy with so much of it, makes me disinclined to criticise the selection of poems. The definition of 'contemporary', at least for the purposes of this volume, starts around 1980 (with Ashbery's 'Paradoxes and Oxymorons') and runs up to Claudia Rankine. Many of the poets are famous, but many others are not, or at least only in small circles. The exhibits stretch from Robert Grenier's one-liner 'shoe from the waves' to four pages of free verse (from Bernadette Mayer and Robyn Schiff) or five of rhyming stanzas (from James Merrill). Anybody with a taste for poetry, however narrow, should find something here to suit them.

Fussy eaters are also likely to find themselves persuaded to enjoy something novel, thanks to Burt's finesse as a host. The essays that accompany the poems are informative, elegantly written, and frequently dazzling in the sensitivity to allusion, form and context they demonstrate. The only issue I would raise perhaps has more to do with the marketing than the substance, but the title's suggestion that the book will be as attentive to the reader as to the texts is misleading. Burt doesn't set out a method or programme for how to read poems, but rather teaches by demonstration. The demonstrations are very entertaining, but as a 'how to' guide it is a bit like trying to learn piano by watching Lang Lang in concert. A reader might be tempted to conclude that, as T. S. Eliot said, 'there is no method except to be very intelligent', not to mention knowledgeable. This is a great volume for filling in, or making one aware of, the gaps in one's knowledge of contemporary poetry; but readers who want to understand exactly how so much can be wrung from such apparently simple or rebarbative poems may feel the need of a supplementary volume that explains the reading skills Burt so brilliantly employs.

Refrains

Karl O'Hanlon, *and now they range* (Guillemot, 2016) £8; Frank Ormsby, *The Parkinson's Poems* (Mariscat, 2016) £6; Geraldine Clarkson, *Dora Incites the Sea-Scribbler to Lament* (smith|doorstop, 2016) £7.50; Zeina Hashem Beck, *There Was and How Much There Was*, smith/doorstop (2016) £7.50; Mark Pajak, *Spitting Distance* (smith|doorstop, 2016) £7.50; Paul Mills, *Out of Deep Time* (Wayleave, 2016) £5; Tom Sastry, *Complicity* (smith|doorstop, 2016) £7.50; Cathy Galvin, *Rough Translation* (Melos Press, 2016) £5; David Gascoyne, *Anniversary Epistle to Allen Ginsberg* (Enitharmon, 2016) £10; *Thirty at Thirty: Celebrating Thirty Years of smith|doorstop Pamphlets,* ed. Ellen McLeod & Susannah Evans (smith|doorstop, 2016) £5

Reviewed by ALISON BRACKENBURY

ONE REFRAIN IN pamphlet publishing is extraordinarily high standards of production. Thanks to Guillemot Press, Karl O'Hanlon's work takes wing from thick, foam-white pages. O'Hanlon's poems display energy, wit and learning, as in his terse account of a scribe of the Anglo-Irish school:

> Of what heats
> stirred among them and caught
> the branches of his script,
>
> running wild through all thought,
> the annals are tight-lipped.

With their 'complexities of hurried light' and compelling rhymes, these are cryptic but rewarding poems. Northern Ireland's conflicts, past and present, are glanced at in refrains rooted in the seventeenth century: '*and the bold boys sang Traitor Lundy*'. These debut poems hold humour in their range: the 'hobby Vikings at Costa'. There can be no objection to terseness when it is as lovely as O'Hanlon's couplet '*The lover and the elegist are one*, / The half-hid truth of the hedgerow's song'.

¶ Frank Ormsby's preface to his poems about Parkinson's Disease stresses that he will refrain from 'the morose, the lachrymose' to write in an 'up-beat strain'. His symptoms are confidently dramatised: 'My left arm is jealous of my right, / the one without a tremor.' Fear of degeneration, an 'answering tremor' in the second arm, runs like a refrain through these poems. Yet so do more hopeful words: 'repairs', 'repaired'.

Even Ormsby's hallucinations, caused by Parkinson's, are compassionate. An imagined spider 'is strangely human and visible all the way'. The poems are often briskly funny: 'Thank you for the list of symptoms. / I have them all.' I was both sobered and cheered by Ormsby's honest humour and recuperative rhymes: 'Assuming I'm alive, / expect an outburst / once a year at least, / a tantrum at seventy, / a rant at seventy-five.' Rant or rhyme, I look forward to it.

¶ That two publishers recently issued pamphlets by Geraldine Clarkson is a tribute to the quality of her work, for which this reviewer's refrain is gratitude. Her new smith|doorstop pamphlet highlights the humour of her Irish heritage: 'Mary Davis stoking up 40 verses / of *The Cleggan Disaster*'. But these litanies of place and people are also movingly reflective: 'Gortín or Mannin / (and I'd thought they were all dead there).' Clarkson's writing has tremendous physical intensity. Her lines on a convent, 'Nuanced at first', end 'volted with pain'. Electricity is her charged refrain, as in the title poem, 'Dora is electric'.

Clarkson is a poet, in her own words, with 'musical bones'. But beside her delicious vowels and verbal arabesques is the respectful insistence that there is 'work to be done', often by women: 'table-linen / in the redhanded grip / of Irish washerwomen'.

The woman speaker in the first poem by Lebanese poet Zeina Hashem Beck hears 'inside my veins […] women, singing'. This poet is a rapt listener to her world. She describes, humorously, her 'color-/coordinated' mother exercising to 'Jane Fone-da'. She preserves, too, final bitter speech: '*Don't name your daughter after me.*'

These are poems unafraid of wider, final reflections. 'God' (often lower case) becomes a refrain: 'Only petty gods want to be worshipped'. Her long title poem, about a weekly meeting, is both quietly eloquent about Lebanese women and touchingly universal: 'I shouldn't, really, / but pass the chocolate'. Its factual ending continues the story of women's work: 'They collect the empty glasses'. The poem's refrain is the pamphlet's title, *There Was and How Much There Was*, a literal translation of the traditional Arabic phrase British readers may know as 'Once upon a time'. This is a powerful, appealing pamphlet, rich with new stories.

¶ Mark Pajak's first pamphlet is dedicated to his parents, 'for all your stories and love'. Its opening poem is dedicated to 'Joe', by whose side the young, drunken speaker dangles off a bridge: 'two boys way past closing time, / holding on until the other lets go'. Years pass between its absorbing couplets. Pajak's stories show shocking shifts. A starved dog found in a shed is not dead: 'he whined / like a knife / scraping a plate'. The short lines are sharp with suffering, although the collie wags his tail.

Pajak's poetry is extreme, its subjects often united with elements and seasons. Camping in a storm, his father is 'counting us / into the eye'. After a brush with a bear, 'my mouth filled with autumn'. Listeners to Mark Pajak's performances, (from memory), will know how his stories' endings haunt the hearer like the close of a dark, irresistible song.

¶ I am haunted too by the last lines of Paul Mills' poems, with their singing alliteration, 'hummed soft in the miles of savannah grass':

> the dead who have gone down into deep time
> starting to come back   beautiful and bone-swift

Writing to a theme, (evolution), however important, may not always suit Mills. But his best writing is marvellously good, with the gift of simplicity. Life comes from 'a wriggle' in time. Poems move towards dialogue: '*think you can wriggle out of it?   see me smile   time said*'. Mills ends with the boldest of declarations, as two gods consider the value of human history: *'will it be worth it? I asked   and you said yes'*.

¶ I especially valued the short poems in Tom Sastry's *Complicity*. Six lines in 'Red Pepper' lead 'A heart with four chambers' to a finale as intense as the best refrain: 'a red red red heart'. Sastry's talent for condensation is demonstrated by the unforgettable 'sludge-mugs' of 'The Office'. His quiet poetry delivers an unexpected political punch: 'The Commission on Nightmares / has proposed a new terror of badgers'. Sastry's own words sum up his pamphlet well: 'There is nothing ordinary about it'.

¶ Cathy Galvin's *Rough Translation* translates ordinary life into elemental cycles, in the swing of short lines: 'In the night / our bodies know. / On the tide / tomorrow. / In the dawn / our hands let go'. I was moved by her deep sense of generations, and by the loving, optimistic tribute to her parents which ends her pamphlet: 'Silenced in life. Believing their children would be heard'.

¶ I am biased towards David Gascoyne's *Anniversary Epistle to Allen Ginsberg*, having heard both poets read. 'Christ of Revolution and of Poetry'...

Gascoyne's strange, compassionate line still echoes in my head, together with Ginsberg's singing of Blake. This prose 'Epistle' is bravely honest about decades of amphetamine addiction: 'Without it I might have written a good deal more'. It can also be very funny, as Gascoyne admits falling asleep during a lecture on Zen: 'I guess I'm allergic to gurus'.

¶ Finally, I recommend *Thirty at Thirty*, with a poem from every year of Poetry Business pamphlets. Here is early work by now-eminent poets, such as Simon Armitage and Daljit Nagra. I wish Nagra's 2003 poem seemed less horribly fresh: his father's vandalised car 'bubbling smarts / of acid'. There are fine poets new to me, including Jeanette Hattersley: 'she noticed one day / her husband had gone / she knitted another / and just carried on'. I was ruefully enchanted by Ed Reiss: 'Who boverns Gritain?' A press like smith/doorstop deserves support by regular buying. This refrain from reviewers has never been truer. Spread the word! Or, like Ed Reiss' Colonel, tight to the Rhymes...

From the Archive

Issue 4, July–September 1978.

JOHN ASHBERY

From John Ashbery's very first contribution to *PN Review*, a selection of four poems that includes 'Pyrography', 'Unctuous Platitudes', and 'The Thief of Poetry'. Fellow contributors to this early issue of the magazine – edited by Michael Schmidt, Donald Davie, and C.H. Sisson – include Eugenio Montale, W. S. Graham, Donald Davie, Andrew Waterman, and Val Warner. Neil Powell reviewed Thom Gunn and Michael Vince reviewed Delmore Schwartz. The annual subscription rate advertised on the first page is £4.50.

A digitisation of the entire *PN Review* archive, beginning with Issue 1 in 1973, is accessible online at www.pnreview.co.uk.

WHAT IS POETRY

The medieval town, with frieze
Of boy scouts from Nagoya? The snow

That came when we wanted it to snow?
Beautiful images? Trying to avoid

Ideas, as in this poem? But we
Go back to them as to a wife, leaving

The mistress we desire? Now they
Will have to believe it

As we believe it. In school
All the thought got combed out:

What was left was like a field,
Shut your eyes, and you can feel it for miles around.

Now open them on a thin vertical path.
It might give us – what? – some flowers soon?

SOME CONTRIBUTORS

Rowland Bagnall is a writer currently based in Oxford. His work has previously appeared in *Poetry London*, *The Quietus*, *Oxford Poetry*, and *PN Review*. **Trevor Barnett** is a teacher of English and he writes about poetry in translation for *PN Review*. He lives in Marbella, Spain. **Sujata Bhatt**'s most recent books from Carcanet are *Collected Poems* (PBS Special Commendation, 2013) and *Poppies in Translation* (PBS Recommendation, 2015). She divides her time between Germany and elsewhere. **Roger Caldwell** is a poet, essayist and critic, living in Essex. He writes on philosophy and literature for various journals. His latest collection of poetry is *Setting Out for the Mad Islands* (Shoestring Press, 2012). **Jay Degenhardt**, born in Manchester and studying at the University of Cambridge, has published poetry in *Stirred Press*, *Notes*, *From the Lighthouse*, and on the Young Poets Network. **Karen Van Dyck** writes on Greek literature, gender and translation. Her poems and translations have appeared in the *Brooklyn Rail*, *Guardian*, *Locomotive*, and *Tender*. **Adam Elgar**'s poetry has appeared in *Poetry Review*, *Stand*, *Warwick*

Review, *Magma*, and other journals. He translates fiction, poetry, art history and psychoanalysis from Italian and French. **Paolo Febbraro** (b. Rome, 1965) is a poet and essayist. His poetry includes *The Diary of Kaspar Hauser* (2003, English translation by Anthony Molino, Negative Capability, 2017), *Il bene materiale* (2008) and *Fuori per l'inverno* (2014), from which the present poems were taken. **Adam Feinstein** is a poet, translator and author of the acclaimed biography *Pablo Neruda: A Passion for Life*, re-issued in an updated edition by Bloomsbury in 2013. It has been translated into a number of languages including Chinese. **Jennie Feldman**'s most recent publication is *Chardin and Rembrandt* (2016), a translation of Marcel Proust's essay. She has two collections of poems, *The Lost Notebook* and *Swift* (Anvil, 2005 and 2012), and has translated Jacques Réda's poetry and prose. **Emily Grosholz**'s *Starry Reckoning: Reference and Analysis in Mathematics and Cosmology* was published in 2016 by Springer, which will publish *Great Circles: The Transits of Mathematics and Poetry* next year. **Jack Hanson** is a graduate student in philosophy of religion. Some of his writing can be found in *The Hopkins Review* and *Open Letters Monthly*. He lives in Chicago. **Shengchi Hsu** is a Ph.D. student in Translation Studies in the Department of English and Comparative Literary Studies at the University of Warwick. **Igor Klikovac** is a Bosnian poet (b. Sarajevo, 1970) living in London since 1993. His work has been published in Bosnia, countries of former Yugoslavia, Britain, and internationally. **Sue Leigh**'s work has been published in magazines and journals including *Areté*, *Oxford Magazine* and the *Times Literary Supplement*. She was a winner of Carol Ann Duffy's Shore to Shore poetry competition (2016). **Maitreyabandhu**'s most recent collection, *Yarn*, is published by Bloodaxe. **Leo Mayer** lives and works in London, where he is completing a postgraduate degree at the London School of Economics & Political Science. **James Leo McAskill** was born in Manchester and studied in Glasgow. He is an editor at Little Island Press. He lives in Lisbon. **John McAuliffe**'s fourth book, *The Way In* (Gallery), was joint winner of the 2016 Michael Hartnett Award. He is working with Igor Klikovac on the translation of his third collection, *Stockholm Syndrome*. **James McGonigal** wrote an award-winning biography of Edwin Morgan, *Beyond the Last Dragon* (2012), and co-edited a Selected Correspondence 1950–2010, *The Midnight Letterbox* (Carcanet Press, 2015). **Drew Milne** is a fellow of Corpus Christi College, Cambridge. The book of his collected poems, *In Darkest Capital*, is forthcoming from Carcanet Press. **John Muckle**'s most recent books are *My Pale Tulip* and *Little White Bull: British Fiction in the Fifties and Sixties*. His new novel *Falling Through* is forthcoming from Shearsman Books. **Miriam Neiger-Fleischmann** was born in Slovakia in 1948 and lives in Jerusalem. She is a painter, scholar, and poet. She and Anthony Rudolf have collaborated on a volume of translations of her work, *Death of the King and Other Poems* (Shoestring Press, forthcoming). **Anthony Rudolf** is the author of *Silent Conversations: A Reader's Life* (Seagull Books/University of Chicago Press, 2013) and *European Hours: Collected Poems* (Carcanet, 2017). He is co-editor of a *Yves Bonnefoy Reader* (Carcanet, 2017). **Carol Rumens**'s most recent collection of poems is *Animal People* (Seren, 2016). **Laura Scott**'s pamphlet *What I Saw* won the Michael Marks Award in 2014 and in 2015 she won the Geoffrey Dearmer prize. **Ian Seed**'s most recent publications are *Identity Papers* (Shearsman, 2016); *The Thief of Talant*, the first translation into English of Pierre Reverdy's *Le Voleur de Talan* (Wakefield Press, 2016); and *Italian Lessons* (LikeThisPress, 2017). **John Upton**'s latest book of poetry is *Embracing The Razor*. He has also had five stage plays produced. **John Wilkinson** teaches at the University of Chicago where he is organising a conference on Gwendolyn Brooks for April 2017. His most recent collection is *Ghost Nets* (Omnidawn, 2016). **Gregory Woods** is the author of *Homintern: How Gay Culture Liberated the Modern World* (Yale University Press, 2016). His most recent poetry chapbook is *Art in Heaven* (Sow's Ear Press, 2016).

——————————————— C O L O P H O N ———————————————

Editors
Michael Schmidt (General)
Luke Allan (Deputy)

Design
Luke Allan
typeset by Little Island Press

Type
PN Review is set in Arnhem, a typeface designed by Fred Smeijers in 1999.

Editorial address
The Editors at the address on the right. Manuscripts cannot be returned unless accompanied by a stamped addressed envelope or international reply coupon.

Subscriptions (6 issues)
individuals: £39/$86
institutions: £49/$105
to: PN Review, Alliance House
30 Cross Street, Manchester
M2 7AQ, UK

Represented by
Compass Independent Publishing
    Services Ltd
Great West House, Great West Road
Brentford TW8 9DF, UK
sales@compass-ips.london

Trade distributors
NBN International
10 Thornbury Road
Plymouth PL6 7PP, UK
orders@nbninternational.com

Copyright
© 2017 Poetry Nation Review
All rights reserved
ISBN 978-1-78410-143-5
ISSN 0144-7076

Supported by